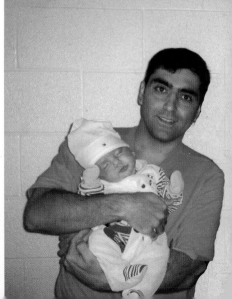

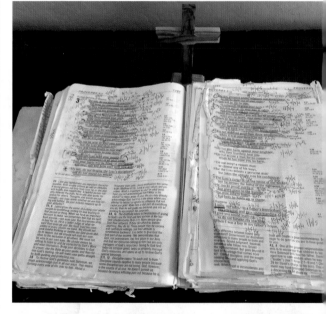

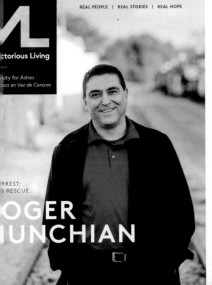

ROGER MUNCHIAN

RESCUED
NOT ARRESTED

RESCUED
NOT ARRESTED

(Revised & Updated)

H. ROGER MUNCHIAN

www.rescuednotarrested.org

Rescued Not Arrested

© 2023 by Roger Munchian

All rights reserved. First edition 2014.

Second edition 2023.

Cover Designer: Jonathan Lewis

Ghostwriter: S. K. Wilkinson

Editor: Paul Miller, Rachel Munchian

Based on the true story written by H. Joseph Gammage

In order to maintain anonymity, the names of some individuals and places have been changed, some dramatic details have been added, and some identifying characteristics and details such as physical properties, occupations and places of residence have been changed.

Published for Rescued Not Arrested by Aneko Press

www.anekopress.com

Aneko Press, Life Sentence Publishing, and our logos are trademarks of

Life Sentence Publishing, Inc.
203 E. Birch Street
P.O. Box 652
Abbotsford, WI 54405

BIOGRAPHY & AUTOBIOGRAPHY / Religious

Paperback ISBN: 978-1-62245-899-8

eBook ISBN: 978-1-62245-906-3

10   9   8   7   6   5   4   3   2

Available where books are sold

Contents

Ministry Information

The concept of a ministry like Rescued Not Arrested, Inc. (RNA) was envisioned by Hrach Roger Munchian while he was still in prison. The ministry today has a no-paid-staff policy to ensure that it is driven by the Holy Spirit's passion – making a difference instead of a dollar and trusting God for all provisions as we serve others globally, especially the least of these in prisons and beyond. Fulfilling Matthew 28:19-20, the Great Commission, is our top priority in life over everything else. Jesus died for us, so we will live for Him. Additionally, RNA's prayers and desires are to challenge the universal church to effectively embrace the formerly incarcerated without categorizing their sins, including the "untouchables" and sex offenders – whom I call the lepers of today's society.

For more information, visit our website at www.rescuednotarrested.org or contact Roger Munchian by email at rogermunchian@ rescuednotarrested.org or by phone at (602) 647-8325. Our mailing address is PO Box 90606, Phoenix, AZ 85066.

My name is Roger Munchian, and this is the story of my life, a life that was broken because I spent my time chasing after money, sex, drugs, and power. However, things changed. I was rescued, restored, delivered, and saved by the mercy and eternal grace and love of Christ Jesus, our Lord and Savior. My life is the story of God's saving grace and how only God could take a mess like mine and turn it into a powerful message of hope to reach the hopeless and helpless around the world. Some of the names have been changed from the earlier biography about me to protect innocent individuals, and some details have been modified or added as needed to write my story, but the main details and overarching story is as true to fact as possible.

Prologue

Early Morning
Thursday, September 25, 1997
Phoenix, Arizona

I heard a cell phone ringing. Then I heard panicked, pleading words. Shuffling footsteps crunched on shattered glass near me, but I couldn't see. I was blind. Nylon fabric, slick from blood and vomit, covered my face. With club-like, powerless hands, I managed to push the airbag away and stared at the smashed windshield.

I turned my head through a drug-like blur and searched for my passengers, trying to speak – but no audible words came out. It didn't matter. The car was empty.

I fumbled at the door handle until I heard it click. Somehow I punched the latch on the seatbelt with my defunct fingers. My legs felt like logs as I dislodged them from the crush of the steering column. I stood, and then I grabbed the car door as my knees buckled. All was quiet now. The wreckage had found its final resting place.

My ears were ringing, my head was throbbing, and I felt a severe stinging in my left eye. I wiped the thick, bloody film from my eye and stepped away from the mangled mess of a car before I collapsed to my knees. I looked up from the glass-strewn pavement.

That's when I saw her – Alma. She was covered in blood, face-down on the pavement with her arms twisted behind her back. Only a short time ago, I held her in my arms as we laughed and danced. Now she lay still and lifeless. I begged, I pleaded, for a sign of life – any sign of life.

Who? And God can stand by and watch. Where did that thought come from? *God, please!*

I stood up on my rubbery legs and tried to call her name, but was met with silence. A rancid taste erupted from my stomach as vodka now tinged with blood burned my throat. I heaved uncontrollably, even after my stomach was empty. I saw visions of Alma alive, then visions of Alma dead – unceasing visions. *God, please!*

Squeezing my eyes shut, I tried to push the nightmare away when I heard a ghastly wailing sound of anguish torturing the night air. Then I realized it was me. Those ungodly sounds came from me.

I forced my eyes open and the nightmare worsened. Maria, another of the three passengers, lay in the shattered glass. She seemed to be looking at me and asking, "Why?" Mere moments ago she had been in the back seat with Benny.

God, help me!

Mechanically, I reached in my blood-soaked pants pocket and pulled out my cell phone. All was a blur. I just needed to dial three numbers.

"Nine-one-one," the voice responded. "This is the 9-1-1 operator. May I help you?"

My trembling hand lifted the phone to my ear. "I . . ."

"Nine-one-one. I hear you, sir. What's your emergency?"

With thick lips, swollen tongue, and raspy voice from bile, I slurred, "I was . . . killed two people. Car accident."

"Sir, what is your location?"

I tried to remember road signs. All that came to mind was 130 mph, and Alma sitting next to me. *God, help me!*

"You said there were fatalities?"

I nodded. "Help. Send help."

"Are you injured, sir?"

I hung up. *Am I hurt? Why am I not hurt? I should be dead – like them.*

My eyes turned to the wreckage – a crumpled heap in the road. Then I looked at Alma. She was lying in a forever sleep on a cold, shard-covered asphalt slab. It was a violent end for her, and the beginning of a nightmare for me.

Tears cleaned the blood from my eyelids. My body trembled. My muscles tightened and squeezed, and pain shot through my leg. Pain – a sign of life – a life I did not deserve. I searched for my .357 to end this pain, but instead I found a Heineken bottle. It was Benny's bottle.

Benny! The third passenger. *Where's Benny?*

With the image of Benny's terror-stricken face emblazoned in my mind from that last moment, I continued my search. Hair, blood, and carnage. I found my briefcase that contained the contracts, a pen, a legal pad, and hundred-dollar bills from a drug transaction – but no gun. When I saw the paper, I knew I had to write a note. People who commit suicide always leave a note, right? I knew they'd have to identify me after I blew my head off.

I scrawled – *Hrach Munchian*

Now what? I added my address. There needed to be more, but what? As a final thought, I wrote, *GOD, HELP ME!*

I tucked the note under the windshield and headed for the bridge, an overpass. The rush of adrenaline and my destiny with death pushed me on.

With overwhelming anguish, I fell to the roadside and cried with an inhuman wailing. I relived that murder scene again: my hands gripping the murder weapon – the car wheel – I was helpless. In a torrent of cries, I recognized only one phrase: *God, help me!*

The images filled my mind – visions of the lives I'd taken in a single drunken moment. I saw that very instant of the screeching impact when the barrier wall turned my precision machinery, the object of my pride and proof of my unquenchable thirst for wealth and power, into a murder weapon and erased two beautiful lives.

God, help me!

Suddenly blue and red lights appeared far down the road. Then came the garbled voices, orders, and commands. I rose to my feet and pushed harder to reach the overpass. I was not fleeing for my life, but was trying to flee to certain death. The blinding spotlight of the helicopter lit my path, but the swirl of dust around me stuck to my blood, sweat, and tears. The dust clung to me, but I was almost at the overpass. I slogged on. Soon it would be over.

I heard more commands – orders to surrender. Not this time. I was only going to surrender to death.

"Stay where you are!"

I was almost there. My heart pounded. I choked for breath. I knew they could not reach me.

"K-9 released!"

As I reached the rail, I heard the snarl of the beast as its razor-sharp fangs grabbed my pant leg. I dragged that dog along, intending to take him with me.

"Stay where you are! Freeze!"

I yanked my leg free and lunged into the air. The rocks and foliage below glowed in the chopper's spotlights as I heaved myself into the air. It was over. *God, help me! God, help me!*

Part 1

God Rescues

Chapter 1

God's Protection

I am an immigrant, an Armenian American, living and working only because of the miraculous protection of God for my family throughout several generations. At the age of eight, I came to the United States of America with my parents to escape the oppression, poverty, and war in Armenia – only to face the gang-infested streets of Los Angeles and Phoenix.

Ironically, in AD 301, Armenia was the first nation to declare Christianity its state religion, but it later suffered under Islamic rule and communist dictatorships. Throughout the centuries, Iran, Ottoman Turkey, and Russia invaded this land and claimed portions for themselves. The Ottoman Empire ruled most of Armenia for several centuries in accordance with Islamic law, so the Christians and Jews had to pay an extra tax for being non-Muslim. In 1915, the rulers of the Ottoman Empire felt threatened by the education and prosperity of the Armenians, so they systematically carried out the second Armenian genocide (the first was in the late nineteenth century). The Turks also resented the loyalty that the Christians had for their "Christian" government, so they rounded up and arrested intellectuals and political and spiritual leaders. Some of these Christians were deported, but most were brutally murdered.

The Turkish government promised my great-grandparents better opportunities and peace, but they only found forced labor camps and death marches – death marches through the desert, where vast numbers of prisoners died of starvation, dehydration, exposure, and disease. Some were cruelly tortured. Others were mercilessly killed. My great-grandparents survived only by the miraculous hand of God, but nearly two million other Armenians were massacred. But my great-grandparents did indeed survive, and they later raised their family, including my grandfather, in Armenia.

To this day, Turkey denies its role in the genocide, but precise documentation of the atrocities, including photos, films, posters, and newspapers, are held underground in the Yerevan Genocide Museum. In the capital city today, purple forget-me-nots (a symbol of genocide) appear on car windows, on walls of shops and offices, and on highway banners with the words "We Remember. We Respect. We Condemn."

Armenia was declared an independent republic in 1918, but it came under Soviet rule in 1922. During the Soviet occupation of this land, the people again suffered. Church attendance was banned and people lived in poverty. Under Stalin's cruel rule, many more Armenian people were killed. My grandparents, Khachik and Elizabeth Munchian, survived and lived through the Second World War, but oppression was fierce and poverty was common. The Stalin regime deceived many of the people, including my grandparents, into moving elsewhere for better opportunities and religious freedom. However, in 1949, my grandparents ended up in the Soviet Gulag system with thousands of other Armenians.

"Gulag" is an acronym for Glavnoye Upravleniye IspraviteIno-Trudovykh Lagerey (Russian for "Chief Administration of Corrective Labor Camps"). The Gulag is a system of Soviet labor camps, detention and transit camps, and prisons. Resistant peasants, purged Communist Party members, military officers, and prisoners of war were all sent to the Gulag. Alexandr Solzhenitsyn claimed that forty to fifty million people served long sentences in the camps between 1928 and 1953. The

Gulag administration compiled their own list of ten million people who served in the camps. The true figures remain unknown.

My dad, Andranik Munchian, was six years old and my Aunt Mara was three years old when they were imprisoned in the Gulag in Siberia. My Aunt Anyia was born there in 1951 during the imprisonment, and two of my dad's sisters died from the lack of nourishment and brutally cold weather.

While in the Gulag, my grandmother met Myranoosh, who became her good friend, but something happened (I do not know what) that likely put her in great danger. My grandmother somehow helped her and probably saved her life. My grandmother's act of kindness and bravery would later be rewarded with a great opportunity for the family.

My father as a boy (on the left)

My family was held captive for five years before being allowed to move to Kazakhstan, and in 1958 they made it back to Charback, a little town near Yerevan, Armenia's capital. Once again, God miraculously protected my family and helped them survive.

As my father grew up, my grandmother played matchmaker and arranged for him to marry Tagui (meaning "queen") while they lived near Yerevan. I was born in that area, very near the majestic, snow-capped Mt. Ararat, where Noah's ark rested. God had miraculously saved Noah's family, and He had miraculously saved my family, too. God had a plan for us.

During my early years in Armenia, my grandfather sold tickets and drove a bus. My dad was a plumber, but all of it was under the communist regime. There was great oppression and no opportunity for advancement. His experience of being in the Gulag, along with the hopelessness of society, led my father to alcohol, which was predictably destructive for him and our family. He became angry and even occasionally beat my mother and me. Life was hard for him, but I could escape to the street with my friends. We played a lot of tag and hide-and-seek. We improvised and often played with sticks and stones and whatever else we could find.

We were what I now call CEO Christians: Christmas, Easter, and Other occasions – because we only went to church on those days. We had a Christmas tree for Christmas, but our poverty was much more extreme than what was considered poverty in the United States. We did not have much at all. We tied apples and socks on the tree to decorate it. We decorated eggs for Easter, but this was spiritually meaningless to us.

Our church building was an old red-brick cathedral. Priests walked around in their robes, and the church building had statues and pictures of saints inside, which gave it an aura of reverence and awe. The church was full of impressive tradition. Candles were lit and parishioners stood and sat ritualistically. It was a lie, though. I knew it even then. The women would be inside the church trying to be holy while the men were outside smoking.

Somehow Myranoosh, my grandmother's friend from the Gulag, managed to get to Los Angeles. Grandma began hounding her every year to submit our names into the lottery for immigrants. Although this continued year after year, Grandma never gave up hope. She persevered like the persistent widow in Luke 18, and God eventually provided through her determination. Our names were at last drawn in 1979, and our whole household (everyone living at our address) qualified to immigrate to the United States. This included my grandparents, my parents, my aunt, my sister, and me.

Having our names chosen was just the beginning of the process. We were broke and we had to borrow money from cousins for travel expenses and plane tickets. We traveled first to Italy, where we received a little support from a church, but had to wait for a month or so before we could fly out to America. When we landed in Los Angeles, I was afraid when I saw so many different people. I hid behind Mama until we saw Grandma's friend and her family. They were the only ones who welcomed us to the United States. We could not speak English, and they spoke broken English. In fact, Myranoosh had misspelled our names on the paperwork, which took quite a while to correct; however, she took us to their home, where we stayed until they could find us a place to rent. Then they washed their hands of us. The debt was paid.

We had made it – but how does a non-English speaking immigrant successfully navigate the foreign land of California? I soon started school. I had only finished first grade in Armenia, but I qualified for third grade in Los Angeles. Along with many other minorities in this low-income community of Los Angeles, I was put in ESL (English as a second language) classes.

We received some welfare until Mama found a job as a waitress. She worked long, exhausting days and only made $2.75 an hour. Dad worked off and on. He was a hard man and had a hard time finding work. He coped with his stress by drinking. Eventually he was hired by a man named Bill to help at his carpet-cleaning business. Sometimes I even helped by hanging flyers on doorknobs to advertise for Bill's business.

Any self-esteem I may have had was shattered at school. I did not fit in because I was so different. I spoke differently and dressed differently, and these things prevented me from fitting in with the others. I wore brown bell-bottom pants, a sweater, and black shoes that were all torn up. Those were the only clothes I had.

In sixth grade I found a good friend – Armen. Armen was also from Armenia. He was the good boy, and I was the troublemaker. We have our differences when it comes to religion and politics, but when I went through challenging times, he always had my best interest in mind. Our families are still friends and share special times together.

At that time, we lived next door to Daisy and Eric. Daisy was a devout Christian who attended a Presbyterian church and Eric was an atheist. They didn't have any children, so they embraced the Munchian children – my sister and me. Daisy invited me to their church's youth camp one year. I was more interested in the girls than in God, but Daisy planted the first seed in me of Jesus being real. She cared and took a personal interest in me. She demonstrated to me what it looked like to be a sincere follower of Christ.

Mr. Reyes was my favorite teacher in school. He was Filipino, and we remained in touch until he passed away. I took school seriously enough to satisfy Mama and Papa. In fact, I was a very good student, getting As and Bs. At least until high school, and where my grades and morals both began eroding. I played both junior varsity and varsity football, basketball, and baseball. I was very athletic and had good things going for me in that area, but the streets were more enticing to me. Without a mentor or guidance from anyone, I was soon caught up in chasing girls and cars. I wanted more and more of what the streets offered. Despite a scholarship from Cal State, Los Angeles, the drug world offered me more hope and financial stability.

My disillusion with the church had grown. I saw people being dragged into church against their will, who then stood outside and smoked after church was over. It felt so superficial, and I didn't understand the pomp and ceremony, all the standing up, sitting down, and everything else. My impression was that there wasn't anything to be gained from it. The service was in Aramaic, and I just didn't take it seriously. As long as my parents could drag me there, I went along; but when I got old enough, I quit. The streets were where I felt a sense of belonging.

Chapter 2

Fleeing Los Angeles

Saturday, June 3, 1989

After I graduated from high school, I picked up a job at Security Pacific Bank in Los Angeles. One Saturday I headed out to work an early morning shift when my pager went off. High demand for quality weed and jacked rides made the pager a better deal than ringing a cash register. I could get anything fast and at a good price. I had all the right contacts: Crips, Bloods, Armenian Power, 18th Street gang, Temple Street gang, and MS. They all had my digits and knew that I could get whatever they wanted since I was well connected to area suppliers who seemed to recognize my potential.

I was $2,200 in debt to my parents for bailing me out of the Burbank County Jail, and although I had a stash of bills in my sock drawer, I didn't feel right paying my parents with money received at the point of my Bulldog .38 caliber. The bills came courtesy of the owners of one Benz and one Beamer who readily "donated" their vehicles when they saw my hardware. I drove each of those cars to my favorite chop shop and got $500 each.

The stint in the county jail that cost me $2,200 resulted from an arrest in Burbank. I had been a straight-A student with an academic scholarship to Cal State, Los Angeles, but a month before my high school graduation, I had my first encounter with the law – which marked the beginning of an eight-year career that would bring me to the door of death row.

The incident that redirected my life involved the disconnecting of a car alarm. My facade as a model student crumbled. Even though I was a stellar student, a varsity jock, and a second-chair violinist with the John Marshall High School orchestra, I struggled with a self-esteem that had been brutalized by the injustices of growing up as an inner-city Armenian immigrant. My father escaped his problems with vodka, and my mother worked wherever she could to keep food on the table. When my homie, Jorge Estrada, introduced me to weed, I found my escape; it felt so good. I learned the rewards of moving hot goods and dealing drugs. I learned the value and experienced the power of packing armor, and I was willing to pull the trigger before the other guy did.

My mistake was working with that idiot Jorge. With a reliable partner standing on the front bumper, I would shatter the window using the white part of a spark plug. Then I would simply reach in and pop the hood. My partner would snip the alarm wires, and I would have the stereo out in seconds. But Jorge was too high on weed to figure out which end of the wire snips to use. He let the car alarm sound too long, and my spotless record had gone down the tubes.

When my pager beeped in the morning, I checked the number, but didn't recognize it. That was a good sign. I thought it was probably a new customer. I dialed the number and heard, "We got unfinished business."

It was Hondo. I recognized the voice immediately. Hondo was a wannabe member of the Armenian Power (AP) street gang. He shared their colors, but not their ethnicity. Though lacking the reputation of the Crips or Bloods, AP was emerging into the major league of gangs with the help of their leader – the brutal Boxer. I had grown up with most of the AP since our families had immigrated at about the same time. Our common experiences of poverty and broken homes pushed most of us into the street life.

The "unfinished business" was the fact that I had flattened him a week before graduation. Hondo and his AP flunkies had been entertaining themselves by picking on another student, a fellow Armenian named Ara. I felt compelled to step in and stand up for Ara. Two hits. I hit Hondo, and Hondo hit the pavement. That made me a hero that day, but Hondo wanted to even the score.

"Hondo, I haven't heard from you for so long! Feels like forever." I tried to divert the conversation.

"You got a lucky shot in. That don't sit so good with me."

"You know, I didn't like the way you were entertaining yourselves."

"You wanna do something about it? You know where we hang. Tonight. No homies. No blades. No irons. Skin on skin. You got it?"

"Name the time."

"Eight o'clock. Sharp."

After I made a smart-aleck remark, I agreed. Hondo promised to separate my eyebrows, and then he hung up.

Hollywood Boulevard

On the corner of Hollywood and Western was Red's Hot Dogs, a shack-like drive-in with a bulletproof Plexiglas patio that sported a sign that said, "Parking in Rear," which I did. Across the street was the Texaco station that the AP claimed as its turf.

I stared at the Bulldog .38 on the passenger seat. *No blades. No irons.* Instinct told me to pack. I was headed straight for AP territory. However, my honor was at stake. My word was my bond. I slid the Bulldog under the seat and got out. I could see the shadows of AP milling around the corner, but I couldn't see Hondo. I spotted the lowrider (the one that chauffeured Hondo) and Hondo's flunky driver, Detox, leaning against the hood and sucking from a bottle wrapped in a crumpled paper sack.

I checked my watch. It was exactly 8 p.m.

When Detox saw me, he pushed himself away from the hood, brushed imaginary crumbs from his hands, then held his hands out, giving me the invitation to come in. The smile on his face told me I should have brought the Bulldog.

"Hey Boxer!" Detox shouted. "We got company!"

The AP moved in to form a horseshoe around me. Boxer was at the tip of the horseshoe and was facing me. He stood with his meaty arms folded. The gothic-lettered AP tattoos were indisputably noticeable.

"You packin', little man?" he asked.

"I'm here to see Hondo."

"Hondo?" My heart sank as I watched him mock me.

"I don't see no Hondo here. You got an appointment?"

The horseshoe tightened, and I knew I was in trouble. Steely knuckles in the ribs from behind propelled me into the kick to my forehead. My heart raced, and the adrenaline surged as I stood my ground, swinging, blocking, and protecting my vital organs as they converged on me like a pack of wolves tearing at their prey. I swung hard and fast, but that only intensified their attack.

Finally, exhausted and unable to lift my arms, I fell to the ground in a fetal position, which allowed several blows to my head and chest. With endless pounding, I felt the world dissolving around me. Then it stopped.

Someone grabbed my hair and yanked my head back. Through my one eye that wasn't yet swollen shut, I saw Hondo and heard the familiar click. The parking lot lights reflected off the blade, and I heard my own voice say "no" as the razor edge came toward my face.

"I'm going to separate that eyebrow for you, just like I promised."

"Slice him, Hondo!" Boxer's voice thundered in my ears.

Slowly the blade came down, but right then, just before the tip reached my forehead, police sirens screamed in the distance as they approached – as if they had been sent from God.

"Drop it, Hondo! Clear out now!" Boxer's voice was my salvation. Hondo's blade clicked shut. The AP scattered. I pulled myself up, but collapsed in the middle of Hollywood Boulevard. Cars flew past me with blaring horns, screeching tires, and blinding headlights. I crawled the rest of the way to my Camaro and squealed into the street, turning left to avoid the screaming black-and-whites that flew past in the opposite direction. I was only a few miles from home, but sitting in a growing pool of blood, I wasn't sure I'd make it. But I did.

My body healed, but it took more than a month for that swollen vein over my left eye to recede. My chest, back, and arms remained an indigo mass of bruises for weeks while three bruised ribs choked every breath I took. My thirst for revenge intensified as hatred festered throughout the summer.

As I prepared for Cal State in September, revenge reared its ugly head every day. I registered for classes, bought my books, and organized my supplies. I also loaded my Uzi and kept it under the front seat of my car. Every night I would detour past the Texaco station with the Uzi on my lap, but I could never pick Hondo out in the group.

On a crisp October evening, I sat with Jorge in the bed of his truck. My ribs were healed enough to get a decent toke on a thick primo joint Jorge had rolled – weed laced with crack cocaine.

"Your offer still good?" I asked Jorge, passing the joint back to him.

"What's that?" Jorge's drug-dazed mind had already forgotten. "What offer?"

I pulled a toke slowly into my lungs and let the smoke absorb. "Like I was telling you, moron. I need some guys. You know, to back me up."

Jorge shook his head. "Oh, the Hondo thing. Wow, man."

"Yeah; wow, man what? Spit it out, moron."

"Wow, man. Don't you, like, think it's over now?"

"Hondo and me, we ain't square yet. I just need some guys behind me so I can get close enough to him to put one between his eyes." I saw Jorge's bloodshot eyes focus on the primo we were smoking.

"So," I said, "you gonna back me on this, or do I gotta go somewhere else?"

Jorge nodded and said, "Yeah. Don't worry. I'll get some guys."

Saturday, October 21, 1989

Jorge got some guys – six members of the White Fence, an LA Chicano gang run by a Chicano named Oso. They were tipping bottles and blowing smoke outside Jorge's truck when I drove up in my Camaro.

"We can get 'em all, man!" a banger named Loco shouted as white powder snorted out of his nostrils like a crazed dragon. He was trouble, and I didn't want him along; but what choice did I have?

Loco pulled out a .22-caliber pistol. "I can pop them easy, man. We blaze through and cut 'em down."

"That's not the way it's gonna happen," I said. "I just need some iron backing me so I can pop Hondo. Nothing happens until Hondo hits the pavement. Understood?"

Loco said, "No way, man! AP goes down tonight! All of them! Down, man!"

Then I got in Loco's face. "You pop off one round, and I sink you in the pavement next. Are we clear on this?"

Oso's second lieutenant, the Lizard, stepped forward. "Don't worry about it," he said to me. "Like you said, it's your gig. Anything goes wrong, I hold you accountable."

I got in my Camaro. The White Fence climbed into the bed of Jorge's truck. When I saw the glow of the Texaco sign, my adrenaline surged. With my sawed-off Savage 12-gauge shotgun under my trench coat, I felt invincible. I spotted the lowrider and roared into the parking lot. The AP reacted fast, taking position as I jumped out of the Camaro. Jorge screeched to a halt, and the White Fence poured out from the truck bed, falling in behind me and fanning out. I got a sick feeling in my stomach when I heard Loco's high-pitched, nervous giggles.

"Where's Hondo?" I called out. I knew I'd have less than a second to pull the trigger before the AP let loose with their lead.

"Right here, hot shot!" Hondo said as he pushed his way through the AP.

Primed and ready when Hondo reached for his gun, I pulled the Savage, pointed it skyward, and pumped it for action.

I still had the barrel pointing high when it happened. Loco's hiccupping giggle went insane, and he charged the AP with gun blazing. In the roar of gunfire, I froze, with the gun barrel still pointing heavenward. Hondo's body twitched and convulsed before going down. With gunfire coming from all directions, I dove over the hood of my car. I heard screams and war cries over the roar of the guns. Looking over the hood, I saw a spray of lead stop Loco in his tracks. His giggle turned into a high-pitched squeal.

Then the shooting stopped. Bodies fled in every direction. As the cordite mist settled, a bloody form emerged and staggered toward me with outstretched arms. It was Loco. His eyes were glazed and dead white as he pleaded for help. Collapsing, he threw his arms over my shoulders. The dying weight nearly pulled me down.

I heard tires squealing and saw the back of Jorge's pickup. Cars raced past in a full-throttled roar. I dragged Loco to the Camaro, and he tumbled into the passenger seat. I punched the accelerator and got out of there. I drove three blocks at 80 mph before I slowed down. Loco's chest was heaving, his lungs were fighting for breath, his mouth was working up and down, and his eyes were pleading – but fading.

"You stupid, stupid, stupid – hack!" I slapped the steering wheel, trying to remember where the nearest hospital was. Where? I knew. I just had to think clearly. "What were you thinking? Just look at you!"

I don't know how I got there, but I saw the sign: EMERGENCY. I pulled into the half-circle drive and hopped out. The triage nurse called for help, but looked confused when I sat the bloody patient down and ran back out. "You're on your own now," I said as the hospital vanished in the distance.

The hours passed slowly. I had gone to a car wash and cleaned Loco's blood off the seat. My pager went off several times. Each call was from Jorge with the tag 9-1-1. Their signal: stay away as long as you can.

I finally headed home around midnight, but when I turned onto my street, a flash of headlights in my rearview mirror caught my eye. I rolled to a stop, and the vehicle pulled in behind me. I reached back and grabbed the Savage. With my finger on the trigger, I pointed the shotgun at the door until I recognized Jorge.

"Man, you gotta get out of here. You gotta go now, Rog!"

"What happened?"

"Loco's dead. Dead! Word got to Oso and the White Fence. They're holding you responsible. Loco took a bullet meant for you. The Lizard told Oso the gig was yours. They been on me all night, asking where you lay your head. They're everywhere looking for your car. The AP, man! Hondo, he'll hunt you down!"

"I saw Hondo go down. No one knows where I live, Jorge. Just keep your mouth shut."

"Man, it's all a mess! We don't know who went down. Just Loco. Now you got Oso and Boxer after you. What are you gonna do?"

My parents were shocked, but not surprised, when I told them I had to leave. Dad sobered up in a hurry as I told a story I thought they'd believe.

"Look, there's no time to argue. I have to go. Tonight. If I stay, if I don't leave now, I'll be dead."

"I'm going with you." The sober words from my father shocked me.

"Dad, no."

"I'm going, Hrach. In Armenia, it's tradition. The father follows the son. Hrach, we do this together." In the spirit of Armenian tradition, like vodka. Always with tradition.

"Where? Where you go?" Mama's heavily accented voice cracked with tears.

"I don't know, Mama. All I know is we can't stay here. We can't stay."

I took the Camaro to my cousin's place and hid it in his garage. We got in Dad's car and headed east on I-10. I could no longer have anything to do with my life in Los Angeles. As we rounded the peak of a hill, I looked in the rearview mirror and saw the lights of downtown Los Angeles as they vanished into a black void. Adrenaline ran through my veins. I hoped it would get us far away from that place – far away.

Chapter 3

Trying a Legit Life

Phoenix

Phoenix was as far as my father and I made it after fleeing LA. Dad was sound asleep in the passenger seat when dawn broke over the Phoenix Valley mountain ranges. I pulled off I-10 for gas and nearly fell asleep filling the tank. When I saw the Motel 6 across the street, I decided we couldn't go any farther.

I made friends fast in Phoenix. They were my kind of people – the party crowd, fast money, and fast chicks. Hot cars with plenty of chrome trim and bumping the sounds, available all along South Central Avenue, helped me fill my social calendar with carnal delight. Despite the temptation to start dealing again, I played it straight. Criminal life had nearly killed me, and I preferred to live.

I came close to jumping back into the game when Nikko, a member of a gang called Dog Town, approached me at a party. He seemed to know or assumed I could score goods. Nikko got right to the point. He was in the market for five kilos of pure scorpion cocaine. I knew I could pull that off with one phone call to my San Pedro connection, but I turned him down. That soured our relationship, which would cause problems later.

After Mama moved to Phoenix, my parents settled into a house in the Northwest Valley. I had a new set of wheels – a Mustang convertible. I went to Westside Insurance to get my car insured, and as I pulled out of the parking lot, I saw a sign tacked to the telephone pole: "Business for Sale. Easy Entry, Great Potential. Call Linda or Kevin at 602 . . ."

I thought this "easy entry, great potential" gig would be a great opportunity for my family and would finally give me a chance to be an honest businessman – a legitimate one this time. I needed something legit to avoid getting sucked into the corrupt way of life with Nikko. I did not want to repeat my LA episodes again, so I dialed Linda to discuss her offer.

As we met with Linda and her son Kevin, goose bumps ran up and down my back. She sucked away at her Virginia Slim, leaving gobs of lipstick on the butt, and Kevin spoke a mile a minute without taking a breath. They were not the people I imagined when I had first seen the sign on the telephone pole. Linda shuffled the paperwork around the kitchen table – real business papers, the kind written and reviewed by lawyers. She picked each one up and squinted at it, then slid them over for us to review and sign.

"Now this is a stand'ud agreement on the payoff of the land contract," Linda said with a heavy New York accent. "The payment is three th-aw-sand a month, as we discussed, you see, and I deduct what's left after interest from the principal. Uh, are you following this, dearie?" She looked at Mama, who stared blankly at the papers while wringing her hands. My father had the same uncertain look in his eyes because neither one knew how to read English.

I stopped Linda and explained to my parents, in Armenian and to the best of my knowledge, the information that was in the documents. "It's called a business agreement. We can't qualify for a business loan, so she is going to be our bank."

"But Hrach, the monthly payment – it's so much," Mama told me.

I showed her the balance sheets and pointed to the revenue number. "Mama, look. Choo-Choo Subs is nicely located right in the middle of a commercial complex. It attracts a great breakfast and lunch crowd because there are few other places to eat. I can work mornings there to keep costs down. Look at those numbers. We can even make extra payments on the balance."

I knew Linda was getting impatient. "I need you to sign and initial, please."

She was pushy and too eager to get her check, and this was my first experience buying a business. I didn't know what I was doing, and I really didn't understand the verbiage on the contract. It was all legal mumbo jumbo in fine print to me. I wanted this done. I wanted a real shot at doing life right because the temptation of fast money was knocking at my door. I grabbed the paperwork and eagerly signed and initialed. Reluctantly, my parents trusted my decision and followed suit. I slid the certified check for twenty grand, my parents' life savings, over to Linda.

She held out her bony hand to shake mine as she said, "Let me be the first to congratulate the new owners of Choo-Choo Subs. Payment is due the first of every month, and I charge a 10 percent late fee for every five days past due."

I averaged three hours of sleep a night during that time. The numbers at the deli the first month were horrible. We were more than two grand short, so I picked up extra hours at my night shift – a security job at UPS. The next month was worse, and I had to borrow on my parents' credit cards to make the payment.

Then one day my friend Mando pushed his way into the deli. He was wearing his flannel shirt buttoned up out-of-line, and his shirttails were hanging out and uneven. That was the uniform of the Hollywood 39th Avenue gangsters. "Man, this place is a morgue," he said as he plopped down near the counter. "Where do you keep the dead bodies?"

"Not in the mood, Mando."

I sacked the sandwich I was making with a bag of chips and tossed it on the counter.

"I was talkin' to my boy Nufo. Man, he thinks you been had on this place."

"What does Nufo know about running a business?"

"All I'm sayin' is he figures this old bat sees a young man and his family fresh off the boat who don't know no better and sells 'em a lemon. Happens all the time."

"Armenians don't come across on boats, moron. Last boat in Armenia was Noah's oversized ark. Nufo's all about smoking pot and chasing girls."

"Hey, he'll hook you up real nice if you wanna get back in the game. The guy can read a bail of weed, that's for sure. A quick look and whiff, and he can tell you the quality and what's in the middle."

The door chimed as a businessman walked in. He paid for the carryout bag and left.

"There's your noon rush," Mando said.

"Shut up."

Mando stood up. "I gotta bolt. You oughta get a lawyer to check the chick out who sold you this joint. Man, I think she saw you comin'."

I suddenly realized the payment was due and wondered what kind of deal Nikko might have. I knew that a couple quick deals could get the family out of the hole. Then I thought about Nufo. He was smart, slick, and was willing to do whatever he needed to for quick cash.

November 1990

I needed sleep bad. Between college courses at Phoenix Community College and working two jobs, I was exhausted. My eyes drooped as I drove northbound on I-17 on my way home from my graveyard shift at UPS. I drove another new vehicle – a gray Nissan pickup that I bought after flipping my Mustang in the desert. Letting another dude drive my wheels so I could sleep wasn't a good idea. He dozed off on I-10 Eastbound, just before Quartzsite, Arizona, and flipped several times into the steep drop-off on the right side of the highway. By some miracle, we survived. I had to be cut out of the Mustang mess with the Jaws of Life after skidding upside down nearly fifty feet on the ragtop. The rescuers were shocked that we weren't decapitated. That was another brush with death, but I never thought to acknowledge God's hand in saving me.

Once again, I was fighting the fatigue. I looked up and saw "Exit Camelback Road." The speedometer was a blur, but it bounced around 80 mph. When I looked back at the road, I was overtaking a Ford F-150 in the middle lane and gaining on it too fast. I tried to quickly swerve, but my head slammed into the steering wheel. I felt my truck twist in the air, and when I looked out the windshield, I saw the wall coming at me. I squeezed my eyes shut and braced for the impact, thinking it would be a miracle to survive another deadly crash.

The Ford spun 180 degrees and came to a rocking halt. The driver stared out his windshield as my Nissan left the road, spun in the air, and crashed through the wire fence on top of the barrier. He reported that he saw the body fly through the windshield as the Nissan skidded across the service drive. He was sure the guy was dead. I was that guy, spared one more time – again not acknowledging God's divine protection.

So now, all battered and banged up, I sat in the insurance office and listened to McFadden, owner of Westside Insurance, attempt to explain a policy to Pablo Cabrera, a non-English-speaking customer. McFadden's bilingual agent was out sick, so I offered to help. I spoke Spanish fluently and put Pablo at ease. We sat at a small, cluttered table, and I went through the policy with Pablo and answered his questions.

In the meantime, McFadden read my accident report again and shook his head. He saw the pictures of the scene. My gray Nissan was a mangled mass of metal. Its wheels were turned heavenward as it rested in the middle of the I-17 service road. Pictures showed debris all over the road: papers, a duffle bag, crumpled fast-food sacks, a security guard uniform, and guns. Lots of guns. There was a hole in the windshield through which I had been ejected. It was a clean hole – not the kind people survive.

After I finished explaining things to Pablo, we shook hands. Pablo smiled, bowed gratefully, and said, "Gracias, gracias."

I limped over to McFadden's desk and sat down in a creaking wooden chair. "Well, you certainly totaled it," McFadden started. He looked at the pictures again. "You got guardian angels watching over you or something? You went through this fencing. If you had hit that vehicle a split second sooner, you would have hit solid wall, and we'd still be peeling what was left of you out of nothing more than a crushed tin can."

I didn't say anything. What could I say? It wasn't good news. I felt the rage rise in me until my hands trembled, and I think McFadden noticed. He was probably thinking about all that hardware I'd been transporting in my truck.

"Roger," he said, "listen. I want to expand my business, but because of this location, most of my clients are Hispanic. My bilingual guy is unreliable. Look, maybe I can offset some things in your claim if you come and work for me here in this office." He grinned to lighten the mood a bit. "Hey, the way you drive, maybe the insurance business is for you." He also told me that he had a lawyer friend who might be able to help me with the deli problem.

December 1990

Jay Andrews was the high-priced lawyer whom McFadden recommended. His office was in one of those downtown high-rise buildings. He had agreed to consult with me about my deli problem as a favor to McFadden. I had spent the previous few weeks learning the ropes of the insurance business from McFadden. Jay stared at my papers, grunting as he flipped through them. After he finished looking through the stack of financials and agreements, he shook his head and removed the spectacles that rested on the tip of his nose.

"Your parents speak English?" Jay asked.

"No. Not much."

"Then they're immigrants. Prey for people like Linda and Kevin."

"Pray for her?"

"No, not *pray*, as in have Jesus save her soul. I mean *prey*, as in an animal pouncing on its food. Come to America. Pursue the American dream. Scabs like Linda watch and wait. She hangs out a sign as bait and usually snags uneducated people. This time she caught a young kid who knows nothing about running a business."

"I'm nineteen. I'll be twenty in a couple of weeks."

"Okay, nineteen. Still young. Big words and numbers. I can tell you're smart."

"Yeah. Smart for a kid."

"I don't get it. Anyway, this Linda bimbo played on your young and eager side. She made the numbers look good, collected the check, and said, 'Congratulations! You're a businessman. You done good for your parents.'"

Jay then pointed to a line item on the paperwork. "See here? That's the signature of her accountant. That's why you thought she was legit, but an independent audit would have shown a very different story. So when you can't keep up with the payments, she gets the deli back and goes after the next victim."

He slid the paperwork across to me. "Contract's solid, son. You could spend a fortune in legal fees to try to get her on fraud, but that's unlikely. Sorry, son. I wish there was more I could do for you."

Chapter 4

Back in the Game

Friday, January 4, 1991

My girlfriend, Angela, had done things up real nice for my twentieth birthday. Her parents' house overflowed with people I knew. She had even hired Sally Tunes, the DJ who had set up jams at the backyard pool. Kegs had been tapped, and my buzz mellowed my rage without taking the edge off my attention.

My anger ran deep after that lawyer gave it to me straight. I'd been had by a Virginia Slim-smoking old bag. Any idiot should have seen that scam coming, but I'd missed it. I moved too fast and missed the details. I loved money and wanted it quickly. I'd played it straight for just over a year. I had played by the rules, kept my nose clean, walked a fine line, and always stayed on what I thought was the right side of the law. What did it get me? Nothing.

It was time to be on the alert, to get on my feet again, and to never trust anyone. I'd start with Nufo. He was two steps away from being on the wrong side of my gun. I felt him watching me a bit too closely all night, as if he was keeping track of how much I was drinking and how many tokes I'd been taking. To throw him off, I had made a few extra trips to the trough, dumping my refilled cup in the nearest planter and hitting the doobie line, but faking the toke.

As the night wore on, I saw Nufo slip out the back door when he thought I was distracted. I followed. He started up the street toward where I had parked my new truck. He acted nervous, as if he sensed someone was watching him. He angled off the sidewalk in the direction opposite my truck and disappeared through a row of hedges. I lost sight of him for a bit, but then I realized he had gone around the block and was approaching my truck from another angle.

I had tried to stay out of the game, but Nufo seemed to be asking for trouble. I had fixed up my new wheels and didn't want anyone messing with them. My truck was a maroon Nissan pickup truck trimmed with chrome deep-dish Dayton wheels. Inside was an Alpine stereo system, and the entire truck gleamed with its custom stripes. A decal of Roger Rabbit on the rear bumper topped it off. My truck was turning heads. It was a magnet for hot chicks, and I was a hit. The really *muy loco* thing was my custom paint job on the tailgate. I had added the letter *I* in front of the word "NISSAN," and an *E* at the end, turning "NISSAN" into "INISSANE" – insane.

When Nufo seemed to be closing in on my truck, I watched him from a distance. I let him slide his slim jim between the door and window. He was good. He had the door open in a second without chipping any paint. He was so quick that the dome light only flashed. I don't know if he was feeling around for the stereo or the secret compartment where I kept cash, dope, and some armor, but he stopped dead in his tracks when the dome light went on and he was looking down the end of my .357 Magnum. I was raging with anger. I had had a tough week, and now this.

I drove with one hand at twelve o'clock on the steering wheel and the other hand resting on my lap, pointing the gun straight at Nufo's chest with my finger on the trigger. Pointing to the passenger seat with the gun barrel, I told him to get up from under the dash.

"Sit down. Buckle up. We're going for a ride."

Nufo's brown face turned dead white. He whimpered. "Oh, man! Is that how you roll? You gonna take me out in the desert somewhere, put a bullet in the back of my head, and leave me face down in the dirt? Man, just do me here, okay? Put me down in my own neighborhood, not out where I'm gonna get eaten up by coyotes."

Nufo carried on for nearly half an hour. I didn't say anything. Eventually he shut up and sat in silence, staring out the windshield. I knew he was scared out of his wits, wondering how far out in the desert I'd take him before planting a slug in his head. Then I spotted some McDonald's golden arches up ahead.

"You hungry?" I asked as I headed for the drive-thru.

"What, you gonna buy me a last meal? Shouldn't it be a steak or something?"

"Best I can do is a Quarter Pounder with Cheese."

"I'd rather have a Big Mac."

We parked in the half-empty lot. Nufo inhaled the last of his Big Mac as his fingers dripped with French-fry grease. Color returned to his face as he hoped that maybe this wasn't going to be his last meal.

"I tried to play it straight. I have tried for more than a year now," I explained as I held my Quarter Pounder with one hand and the pistol with the other. "I could see where the criminal life was leading me. I saw a guy go down from a bullet meant for me, and I still got a serious price on my bean. Now I gotta look over my shoulder in certain places so I don't go down for a permanent nap."

"Where'd this go down?"

"It doesn't matter."

"Sorry."

"I can tell you know how to work all your angles, and you look like you can hold your own. I've seen you dance the ring. Featherweight?"

"Yeah, but I'm looking for a new gym. All I get to train with are flat-footed pugs. I want to get in where my little brother trains, but I don't have his clout. He was a featherweight Olympic contender."

Nufo was jittery. He cautiously pulled a joint from his pocket, not wanting to make any sudden moves. The gun was still pointed at his heart. He blazed it up and offered me a toke, but I waved it away.

"What happens next? You always take guys who try to jack your ride out to dinner? Is this a ritual before you cap them?"

"I have a proposition for you."

"You catch me stealing your stuff, you drive me out here, and now you wanna cut a deal? Sounds insane to me."

I was feeling insane. I was ready to go all out to rebuild my network. That deal with Linda burned me bad. Never again.

"First, let's get something straight. No one messes with me, Nufo. You got that? No one messes with my truck. No one messes with my stuff. You've been working an angle, trying to get close to me, trying to find out where I lay my head, looking to jack my stuff. You made your play tonight, and it could have gone way different for you. Got that? You're better than most, but you ain't good enough. Maybe you can work for me making serious dough instead of chasing pennies stealing rims and stereos."

"I don't know where to score big."

"Nufo, you're good, but you need a leader to guide you to better things. You move and jab real good in the ring, but on the street, you need experience and good suppliers."

"So what do you have in mind?"

"I understand you have a nose for quality weed."

"Yeah, I know my stuff."

"I don't mess much with coke and meth."

"Good profit in both."

"Meth rots your face away, and I saw a guy die taking a hit of crack cocaine. No thanks. A little crack to lace my weed for a Primo joint is the best, and that's all folks."

I explained that I needed to put a supply base together for marijuana but wanted to stay clear of old LA connections. "I want a reputation for supplying good stuff fast, and I need a good quality manager to pull that off."

Then I asked him if he moved goods. His eyes lit up. "I do VCRs, stereos, wheels. Sometimes jewelry, but I don't like stores so much.

Cops respond faster to an alarm at a jewelry store. Blockbusters are my best target. In and out in fifteen minutes. Cops take twenty."

We talked about how many times a week we could pull it off. Nufo was a bit shocked when I suggested every night. I could tell he was thinking hard.

"Here's how we do it. We set up a pager system, a numbering code. Say I end a call in something like '9-5'; that means I got an order for five VCRs. A nine means VCR, and five is the quantity. If I start with an eight, it means car stereos. Six – mag wheels. Five – an Eldorado . . ."

"Eldorado! What? You want me to break into a Cadillac dealership? Drive the car through the showroom window?"

"You never jacked a car? Roadside, take it at gunpoint – not hot-wiring it from some lot at night."

"No. Never."

"It's a good trade to learn. How do you handle a gun?"

"I'm better with my fists."

"You're gonna have to learn to handle hardware. Even if you're not a good shot, you can still convince someone they are risking a case of lead poisoning. You on board?"

Nufo chucked his Big Mac wrapper out the window and held out his greasy hand. "When do we begin?"

"School's in session."

May 1991

Gang-related shootings had increased along the interstates running from South Central Phoenix, so several unmarked units had earned special detail on the I-10 corridor. As I passed one of them in my Nissan, going 80 mph, they spotted me right away. They followed me without flashers for several miles while one officer tried to run the plate on the truck. No luck.

I exited and merged onto southbound I-17, still running at 80 mph. Before long, they hit the lights, so I slowed down and moved over to the right lane. I then pulled to the side of the road and slid the back window open to air the cab out as one officer approached on the left, and the other on the right. The one on the left walked with his hand resting on his holstered gun, with the strap unclipped. I slowly opened the door, and the dome light lit up the interior.

"I'm Officer Arnett, and he's Officer Miller."

Miller was doing a lot of sniffing. He inspected my cab and found various papers and my black gym bag with my name on it, while Arnett walked me to the back of the truck.

"I'm a student at Phoenix Community College, and I work several jobs," I explained. "I'm in a hurry to pick up my mother and sister from Sky Harbor Airport. They're coming in on the 11:45 flight from LA."

"You've got an hour," Miller said. "Gym bag says 'Roger Munchian.' That you?"

"Yes."

"Mr. Munchian, I smelled marijuana coming from your vehicle. You want to tell me why that would be?"

"I don't know, officer."

"You mind if I search your gym bag?"

"I'd rather you didn't."

"Okay. We'll wait for the canine unit to arrive."

As Miller lifted the bag from the floor, he saw the stock of a gun wedged between the driver's seat and floorboard, positioned for easy access. He retrieved it. It was a 12-gauge, sawed-off shotgun that had been specially fitted with a pistol grip. He broke it open and saw that it was loaded. He carried it to the back of the truck and said, "Mr. Munchian, you are under arrest for possession of a deadly weapon, concealed within immediate control."

Then they spun me around and frisked me. They found two pagers in my pocket, both buzzing. Then Miller unzipped my bag and pulled out school papers, a calculator, insurance papers, and two plastic Ziploc bags filled with about a half-pound of marijuana.

"Add possession of marijuana to the charges. Not your night, is it, Munchian?"

Arnett put me in cuffs, and Miller went back to the cab to inventory my belongings before the tow truck came. He found my wallet, a loaded .44-caliber blue-steel snub-nose revolver, a holstered .25-caliber semi-automatic handgun with a box of ammunition, a plastic container with two white rocky substances, another Ziploc bag with white powder, and a loaded stainless steel .357 revolver, unholstered.

The field test on the white powder was positive for cocaine, so Miller said, "Here's what we're looking at, Mr. Roger Rabbit: possession of a narcotic drug for sale, possession of marijuana for sale, narcotics trafficking while in possession of a deadly weapon, possession of a prohibited weapon, and carrying a deadly weapon within immediate control."

As I was being led away, Miller called out, "Mr. Munchian, if you give me your mother's flight number, I'll let her know you'll be late – about ten to fifteen years late."

Chapter 5

Trouble at Choo-Choo's

Iknew I wasn't popular yet with Sally Tunes, but I needed a top-notch DJ for my plans for Choo-Choo's. I wanted to open up the sub shop for an underground place to party and jam after hours. I figured I could charge top dollar to get in for "drinks all night" and hot babes in miniskirts. The dudes would pay prime to get in on that.

I walked into Sal's studio to make the proposition. "Hey, Sal. That gig you did for my birthday was the best."

"Yeah. I try to keep my reputation up."

"Well, I can help you out there. I'm thinking of opening up the sub place for after-hours parties. I need the best. That's you. I want you exclusively, Friday through Sunday nights."

Tino was sitting with Sal and turned white as a sheet. "I don't know about this deal, Sal. Man, if he opens that place up, he's gonna have the Brown Pride, VTC, Westside Chicanos, Vista Bloods, Dog Town, Hollywood 39, all of them bangers in the same place at the same time. That's a bloodbath waiting to happen."

"Don't matter, Tino. I'm booked," Sal said as he pretended to look at his schedule.

"How far out you booked?" I asked him.

"For the rest of my life," the smart aleck smirked.

That struck a nerve, and the challenge was on, so I kindly asked him to recheck and look a little closer. He pretended to look again and said, "Nope. All booked."

"Look again," I told him as I held my nickel-plated revolver to his forehead and pressed a red dot right in the middle.

"Oh, look. Here's an opening," Sal blurted out. He was suddenly very excited to have regular gigs every weekend.

September 24, 1991

"You gotta be kiddin' me," Mando said. "Just dropped it, huh?"

"They used the word *scratched*," I said. "I guess it means they dropped all charges."

I was behind the wheel of Roger Rabbit, and Mando was in the passenger seat as we watched my girl Jenny get information from the Dog Town homies. Nikko had called and invited me up to his crib. He said he knew where he could get some quality weed of serious weight. I didn't believe him. He was up to something. I really wanted to get back to Choo-Choo's. I had left Nufo in charge and brought Mando along for extra muscle. Dog Town and Hollywood 39 didn't mix well, so I brought Jenny along as a neutral party.

Moving the dope was bringing in enough cash to stay current with payments to Linda, but I wanted to keep some proceeds for myself. While waiting for Jenny, I told Mando about my arrest at Sheriff Joe Arpaio's Madison Street Jail.

"They moved me around all night from one cell to another through the intake area called the Horseshoe. It took more than a week to wash the stench of stale urine and sweat off me once I got out. I finally got in front of a judge, and now I owe $2,500 to Arizona Bail Bonds. Had to use Choo-Choo's as collateral."

"That's tough, man."

"Yeah, but a few weeks later as I was waiting for a court date, I got notice that the case had been scratched. No court date."

"You mean the State just dissed your case? They ain't comin' for you?"

"That's the way it appears."

"Hey, man, that's just messed up. Something ain't right. Scratched? I ain't buyin' it. You get pulled over by a couple unmarked narcs? For speeding? Those guys ridin' unmarked don't do traffic stops. Something ain't right. They're on to you. Better lay low. Cut it for a while. Something ain't right."

"Something ain't right out there either." I looked through the windshield and saw Nikko with four of his homies getting in Jenny's face. I reached over, popped the glove box, pulled out a .25-caliber Beretta, and handed it to Mando. "Keep this handy."

I could see that Nikko was irate, ranting and flashing his gang signs. Then Jenny came running. I reached under the front seat and grabbed my Uzi. "Let's do this."

We stepped out of the truck. I shielded myself behind the open door, and Jenny crawled onto the front seat. Nikko moved closer and shouted, "Hey, Roger Rabbit! What 'chew doing bringing a Thirty-Niner across the Dog Town set?"

"Nikko, you're the one who dialed *my* digits. You got something happening? If not, we're leaving."

Nikko and his homies moved to block the road. The road behind me ended in a cul-de-sac. The only way out was through the Dog Town boys.

"Yeah, you can get out of here. No problem. On foot. You leave the truck. I'll take it as toll for bringing the Thirty-Niner across my set."

"No one messes with my truck, Nikko. You know that."

"Not your truck no more," said Nikko's second lieutenant, Joey. "Wheels belong to Nikko now."

They started moving toward us, so Mando stepped forward to the front of the truck. He raised the Beretta and fired three blasts into the air. The Dog Town boys continued their advance, more determined this time.

"Mando," I shouted. "*Never* pull a gun unless you mean business!" I pulled out the Uzi and squeezed off a blast, then laid out another spray. Blue smoke filled the air. The Dog Town boys scattered. Sparks flew and car windows shattered. After the breeze whisked the smoke away, the road was clear.

"Get in!" I shouted, and I hopped in and cranked the ignition.

"Man!" Mando shouted at me as I floored it to 80 mph in no time. "I just wanted to scatter them."

"My way was more effective. No one messes with my truck."

When I saw the red and blue flashers in the rearview mirror, I pushed the accelerator to the floor. I lost the cop, but I knew it was only temporary. I turned down a narrow alley and screeched to a stop next to a trash bin. I popped open the door, but heard the sirens closing in.

"Both of you – get out!" I grabbed the guns and tossed them into the dumpster. "Mando, your apartment is two blocks from here. I'll meet up with you both there. Take the back way. No streets."

I jumped back into the truck, but as soon as I left the alley, two cruisers were on my tail. I tried to get as far away from that alley as I could. Four police cruisers were on me, and a copter dropped down from above. With the blinding lights all around, I lost control, hopped a curb, and skidded to a stop in a parking lot. Armed officers scrambled for position, and I could sense their guns drawn on me from behind open car doors. What really scared me, though, was the glint of a sniper rifle from the open door of the copter.

"Throw out your weapons and put your hands on your head!"

I rolled down the window and held my arms out, realizing that the intensity of the situation could mean a bullet to my forehead any second.

"I'm unarmed!" I shouted. "Don't shoot! Don't shoot!"

"Mr. Munchian, this is your final warning. Throw your weapons out and exit the vehicle."

"Please!" I waved my arms. "I don't have any weapons! I'm unarmed."

I popped the door open and fell to the ground with my hands on my head. Police converged on me and slammed my face into the pavement. I felt the cold steel cuffs clamping onto my wrists.

"I'm unarmed!"

They yanked me to my feet and threw me into the back seat of the patrol car. I watched through the wire mesh as the officers converged on Roger Rabbit. I could only hope that I had dumped all the weapons, but it had been so hurried and frantic that I wasn't sure.

Choo-Choo Subs
Sunday, January 4, 1992

Almost three months had passed since that night, and I waited in the rear parking lot behind Choo-Choo's for Nufo. I leaned against the bed of Roger Rabbit and packed a tight joint. Nufo pushed through the back door carrying two Styrofoam cups of beer. I had dressed casual in sweats and a baseball cap; it was my birthday, after all.

"Happy Birthday, inmate #T380626."

I grabbed the beer. "Not funny, Nufo."

"Hey, how'd they get something on you?"

"I was confident I'd walk free, even while I sat in the Madison Street zoo getting my booking number. Without the weapons, they couldn't nail me on anything, but Mando blew the whole thing. While I waited my turn before the judge, the cops found Mando and Jenny. Mando freaked out and spilled his guts. He even told them where the guns were. By the time I got before the judge, the gun issue had been added to the case, so I got charged with aggravated assault with a deadly weapon. I couldn't get bail until morning, so I spent a night in that zoo. I had to put Choo-Choo's up as collateral again, but I was out by five."

"You get a trial date set?"

"Heard nothing so far."

"Hey, maybe they scratched this one too. Man, Rog, sometimes I think you got major weight in heaven. You have guardian angels with serious clout watching over you."

I thought about that. No indictments had come down, and I was looking at five counts of aggravated assault at ten years a pop. That would mean I'd spend the next fifty years living in orange at ADOC (Arizona Department of Corrections) – maybe more if the drug charges came up again.

I noticed that the music had stopped. Sal was taking a break between sets. "Things still looking rough in there?" I asked Nufo.

"Yeah. West Side Chicano (WSC) boys been lookin' for trouble all night. Williams and Bokowski are with them. Gilbert already tossed Louie out three times. He kept trying to pack his .22. Then some Tolleson VC boys showed up, and they've been talkin' trash."

"Eddie in the mix?"

"Not yet. Gilbert's been trying to keep a buffer in there, but yeah, things are getting hot."

"Let's get the party to wind down. How's the kegger?"

"About half full. You really got a bad feeling about tonight?"

"Once the kegger's gone, pull the plug on Sally D and get everybody out."

I moved back inside and soon saw the Tolleson boys come through the front door. Gilbert gave them a heavy pat down, but my gut feeling had been correct. I saw it coming, but it happened too fast to do anything. It started with a fistfight on the dance floor. Sally D's tunes stopped, and we heard gunshots coming from the parking lot. I grabbed the mic and announced that the party was over.

When I turned around, I saw Williams push his way through the door and take aim at Eddie. That's when I heard Bokowski scream, "I've been shot!"

Gunfire engulfed the parking lot as the Tolleson boys tried to take out the WSCs. Then I heard, "Eddie's been shot! Eddie's been shot!" Eddie was just a too-anxious sixteen-year-old. His fellow gangbangers loaded his limp body into their white Impala and shot their way out of the lot.

Three days later, I had an appointment at police headquarters downtown for more questioning about the shooting. Wearing a shirt and tie did not help my disposition. I glanced down at the *Arizona Republic*, which was still folded to the headline:

One Killed, One Injured in Gang Fight

Phoenix, Jan. 6 – A fistfight that escalated into a shooting spree between two gangs left a 16-year-old dead and a man critically wounded early Sunday in West Phoenix, authorities said.

Edward Chavez, 16, believed to have been from the Tolleson area, was killed in a flurry of shots fired about 12:15 a.m. outside Choo-Choo's Subs, said Sgt. Chester Robertson, a Phoenix police spokesman.

Robertson said people were attending a dance party inside the shop when a fight outside turned into a gun battle. Several types of weapons were used . . . .

The gangs, which police declined to identify, have been feuding for about a year, Robertson said. No arrests had been made as of late Sunday.

I was irritated that the police investigators were taking their own sweet time doing the investigation. Choo-Choo's was still roped off in yellow police tape. It didn't really matter when they told us it was okay to reopen because the closure and the end of late-night blowouts had already put my family in default with Linda. Eddie lost his life. My parents lost their business.

I checked the time. I had to go, no matter how much I dreaded this next step. In addition to the questioning of dozens of Choo-Choo's guests that night and a flurry of other related investigation activity, a Superior Court judge had finally signed an arrest warrant from a grand jury indictment that had sat on his desk for two months:

Warrant for Arrest: Hrach Roger Munchian

To all peace officers of the state of Arizona:

An indictment has been filed in this court against above-named defendant charging that on or about the 24th day of Sept. 1991, the crimes of Aggravated Assault, counts 1 through 5, a class 3 felony and serving alcohol to minors, 1 count, a class 6 felony.

The court has found reasonable cause to believe that such offenses were committed and that the defendant will not appear in response to summons, or that a warrant is otherwise appropriate.

You are therefore commanded to arrest the defendant and bring said defendant before this court to answer for the charges.

Chapter 6

Tent City

Maricopa County Jail
September 1993

I was one of the lucky ones. I observed the veteran inmates rolling their thin mattresses at the head of the bed and securing them with the loose end of their pink sheets. This provided a pillow, but also kept the sheet from falling to the ground, which would allow the rats to climb onto the beds. The first thing they went for was your face.

Unfortunately, my former cellmate, Martin, had learned the hard way. On our third night, he woke the whole tent up with horrific screams when he awoke to a rat biting him. He screamed and bled all over the bunk. The other inmates got rid of the rat. Martin got three days in the infirmary.

On this particular morning, I woke to the voice from the speakers that swayed from the tent pole in the middle of the compound. Wearing my prison-striped bottoms and pink flannel undershirt, I slipped on my orange slippers and grabbed my striped top. Outside the tent, a cool breeze from the west was finally cooling down the scorching temperatures of the Phoenix summer. I was thankful that one summer of this was all I had to endure, and I was approaching the last month of my one-year stretch in County.

I had actually been stopped for a traffic violation on January 14, and when they ran my plates, they discovered there was a warrant out for my arrest for aggravated assault. I stood there handcuffed as they inventoried my truck and confiscated my Chinese-made Norinco 9mm, along with all nine rounds and my Davis .38 caliber. They tucked me into the back of the cruiser, and I was soon back at Madison Street Jail going through the booking. Good ol' Choo-Choo's still worked as collateral for bond.

That's when the court fight began. Mando was right. My cases had never been scratched, as in wiped off the books. They had been preserved, like savings bonds, becoming more valuable to the district attorney as more charges were racked up. They put my assault and marijuana charges together and told me I was looking at a "couple of dimes' worth" – twenty years – as a personal guest of the Arizona state prison system.

After eight months of court battles, I pled *nolo contendere* to all counts, accepting a plea of twelve months' county jail time and four years of IPS-intense probation. Pooling my charges made the state's case stronger, and my attorney discouraged a jury trial. He told me, "This is the way the state plays ball with guys like you, Rog. They stick your charges in a little savings account, so to speak, and then dump it all on you later for leverage on a plea agreement. They get you to plea so you don't fight your case in fear of losing the trial and serving the max sentence."

My sentence began on October 16, 1992, in Estrella County Jail. I argued that I had a business to run, so I qualified for work furlough. When my time was about up, Tent City opened. It was built from a bundle of Korean War surplus tents that Sheriff Joe obtained. I was one of the first of Joe's happy campers and was looking forward to my release in a month.

My other Tent City cellmate was Rizzo. He had been transferred from Durango Jail, and I didn't care much for him. However, after Martin was sent to Madison Street Jail for fighting, I got to know him a little better. The day we were locked down, Rizzo told me all about himself, and he blamed his partner, Miguel, for the whole fiasco.

"See, Miguel – he was the one responsible for packing up the suitcases. I was only to carry them and buy tickets. Miguel picked the stuff up and packed it, but he wasn't smart enough to line the suitcases with something, you know, to throw the dogs off."

"Would you have been?" I asked.

Rizzo thought for a minute and then said, "No, I guess not. They booked me in at Durango Jail where I sat until I could get Uncle Vinnie to put up $3,500 for bail. Then I played their court games for two months."

"Where's Miguel now?"

"Over in Towers Jail. He's got priors and is looking at doing time at ADOC. Me, I got six months here, work release, and then one year of probation. I gotta do probation here. I can't go back to Cali. My girl Paulette picks me up and takes me to my pool-cleaning job. Without her, I'd violate, not able to get to my job. They'd toss me back in Durango. Some guys there didn't like me much. Now she's talking about going back to Cali, and I won't have a ride. Then it's back to Durango. I can't go back there, man. Not even for a day."

"So buy yourself a junker and drive yourself."

"Got no money, man."

"You know, you find a lot of excuses for making life tough on yourself."

Rizzo then sobbed about his recent problems in California with a divorce and two children. He told me that his mother abused him and that he had attempted suicide. Hospital bills piled up, so he thought he could do one or two runs for Vinnie and be clear. The guy was a perpetual loser, and I knew it.

Work furlough gave me time to think of nothing but building a solid business. Every morning, McFadden smiled – probably because I, his jailbird employee, was producing new sales. I was grateful that he had given me the opportunity to work for him even after I was arrested. He worried all the time about everybody else and loved making money. He was gone a lot trying to boost business throughout the Valley, but when he returned to the office, he was melancholy and worked a lot. Then he'd lock himself in his office, and I wouldn't see him for the rest of the day.

One night I returned to the jail at curfew time and joined the line of Joe's happy campers waiting to get processed back in. Rizzo pushed his way over to me.

"You look like death warmed over," I told him.

"I'm going back to the hole, man. Durango, the stink hole."

"What happened?"

"Paulette's leaving. Going back to Cali."

"You're getting out in a month. It's not like you're gonna be sitting in the hole forever. Quiet time might be good."

"Roger, didn't you listen to me the other day? I've got problems with people there. I won't last a week."

The processing line moved forward. I hoped the interruption would end the conversation. No such luck. Rizzo caught up to me and continued his moaning. "The only solution is if I can buy that truck I was telling you about. But I ain't got the five hundred bucks."

"You could ask for protective custody."

"Man, I can't handle that. No way."

I grabbed a book, crawled into my bunk, and pretended to read. Rizzo sat on his bunk and stared at the floor.

"If I could just come up with the dough for that pickup."

I closed my book and said, "Why don't you just get to it and ask me, Rizzo?"

"Uh – you got five hundred bucks you could float me – just until I pay you back?"

He looked so pathetic, terrified about going back to Durango. I suspected he wouldn't survive lockdown, and they would find him dangling at the end of his bedsheets tied to the second-floor rail.

"Okay. You show up at the insurance place tomorrow, and I'll float you a loan."

The next morning, I saw Rizzo and Paulette turn into the parking lot in a rusted-out maroon Impala. They came in all smiles, and he introduced me to Paulette. I gave him the five hundred in cash, and they left. I didn't expect to ever see that money again. As it turned out, it would have been better if I hadn't.

Tucson, Arizona
February 1996

"The way I see it, you owe me more than a hundred grand." Rizzo was trying to talk tough as we sat at an open-air bar in Tucson. He had a proposition, but his ideas never panned out.

He had eventually returned to repay the $500 he had borrowed. About a year later, he showed up all decked out in gold and driving new wheels. It looked as if Rizzo expanded while I had spent the previous year keeping straight and sticking to my probation.

As usual, he spilled all the details. He had started running loads of weed to Uncle Vinnie's customers all over the country, moving major weight and collecting $10,000 per load. Then he picked up some customers of his own. His best customer was some guy up in Detroit they called Robbie the Jew. It was a wonder he lived past his first load to Robbie.

Rizzo had secured a bundle of high-quality skunk weed from Carlos, his connection in Mexico, and had driven it himself to Detroit in February. He was supposed to meet Robbie, but when he got there, he was met by a big guy named Bo, one of Robbie's flunkies. Bo seemed overly eager to check out the load by himself, but Rizzo insisted on going with him. Bo didn't like the quality, so he only offered him half of what he had agreed with Carlos. Rizzo called Carlos and got Carlos to agree to the offer.

When Rizzo got back to Tucson, Carlos was waiting for him. Rizzo gave him the cash, expecting Carlos to peel off the ten-thousand-dollar payment and give it to him for his cut as usual. However, Carlos took everything and told Rizzo that he owed him more than fifty grand to make up the difference. When Rizzo didn't understand, Carlos explained that he expected a certain margin out of every deal, and his guys had to make up the difference whenever the load fell short. Rizzo had just begun to protest when he experienced a set of brass knuckles that shut his mouth for a month. Rizzo told me that he had quit running for Uncle Vinnie and was focusing on getting customers.

At that point, he peeled off $500 from a wad of bills that I'm sure he wanted me to see. I was sure he had an ulterior motive in all the drama. He always had an angle. True to form, this time he wanted in on the insurance business, and he asked me if McFadden had franchising opportunities. He wanted to set up a branch down in Tucson and start something legit. I knew he needed a way to launder his dope money.

McFadden wanted a hundred grand to start the franchise. Rizzo plopped it down, in cash, and McFadden had me oversee the new Tucson operation. That was a lot closer to Rizzo than I ever wanted to be.

Rizzo never made a dime on his investment. Paulette ran the operation. I made regular trips down there to show Paulette how to make it work. She became a basket case, and the branch was sinking. Rizzo was always too doped on his own supply to notice.

Then McFadden announced he was bankrupt. It finally made sense – McFadden's battle with greed, chasing that money no matter how it came, his perpetual meetings with his bankers, and his crazy around-the-clock schedule. The Tucson operations were liquidated along with everything else.

When I showed up with the "Out of Business" signs, Rizzo started talking trash. He grabbed his phone to let me know he was calling some of his people to have them go pop McFadden. I walked back to my car and grabbed my holstered 9mm. It was the first time since the start of probation that my finger curled around the trigger. A rush of adrenaline fill me. He was on the phone when I went back in. I walked up to him with my gun in my hand. "Lighten up, buddy," I said.

He put the phone down without even saying goodbye. Just then Paulette walked in, so he tried to act tough, but his voice squeaked when he said, "Get out. You and me – we're done."

I walked out, holding the gun at my side. I felt it again – that power surge that came from pinning a guy down at gunpoint, the feeling of control over life and death. It was more powerful than any drug. Once again, I had tried to play it straight. I thought that a year in the Tents would have done the trick. I had been certain – until the power surge came when I dotted Rizzo's head with the gun barrel.

I missed that godlike feeling – the power to be in control again that only came from handling the business end of a gun.

Trying harder to stay legit this time around and not get sucked back into the corrupt world, I decided to keep my insurance clients, and I talked my parents into using the west-side location in South Phoenix to open our own insurance business. I still felt guilty for what had happened to Choo-Choo's. We renamed the business "Diamondback Insurance" and went to work. My probation kept me focused and out of trouble for another six months, but then Rizzo called. He wanted a meeting in Tucson. I packed the 9mm, reigniting the power surge that I once again craved.

That explains how I was meeting with Rizzo again after more than three years out of the Tents. Rizzo got right to the point, reminding me of how much money he had lost in the insurance deal. "You cost me a hundred grand," he said.

"Rizzo, it was an investment, okay? Sometimes you win; sometimes you lose. You take a risk."

"I don't believe you didn't know the old guy was having problems."

"No, I didn't know. What do you want me to do?"

He sat there a long time, pretending to think. I knew he had something up his sleeve. "I got some drivers running product for me. I want to try a couple new routes to get new customers, but I gotta take care of Robbie the Jew in Detroit. He's gonna get ticked off if I don't keep his product flowing."

"What kind of product are you talking about?"

"Between four and five hundred pounds of weed per load. Weed – all wrapped and in duffel bags. All you do is slip behind the wheel of my Suburban, drive to Detroit, and make the drop. Make sure the Jew don't try to stiff you like he did me. Bo's the guy you gotta watch out for. I pay ten to fifteen grand for the Detroit run. You do five straight for me and I'll call the debt even."

I suddenly felt the rush that I hadn't felt in a long time. First the gun in my hand when I dotted Rizzo's head, and now this. It felt good. Money and power were once again within my grasp. I knew Rizzo wouldn't last long at this. He was clumsy and lazy, but I sensed that I could get in on something before his luck ran out.

"If you run your dope business the way you ran your insurance business, you and I are going to have serious problems down the road, you got that? I only warn you once. I'll check it out. If I sense anything wrong or out of line, I'll come back with the product and pop a cap right dead center in the middle of that forehead of yours. Understand?"

"You threatening me?"

"No, Rizzo, it's a promise. No one messes with me. No one messes with my stuff. I'll do this for you, but if you try to screw me, you're dead."

We shook hands. Rizzo's hand was cold and clammy, but the deal was made.

Hrach "Roger Rabbit" Munchian feeling the rush of power – I was back in business.

Chapter 7

New Connections

Detroit
February 1996

I pulled into the parking garage of the Detroit Omni Hotel, knowing that Robbie the Jew wanted me to park the Suburban at a parking meter five blocks away. In the back seats and storage area were duffel bags full of tightly wrapped bales of marijuana – two hundred pounds. I parked in the closest spot to the elevator.

I walked into the luxurious lobby and checked my watch. I was fifteen minutes late. Perfect. That gave me a chance to scope out trouble. From the front desk, I had a view of the lounge and the bar. I saw businessmen and tired women, but no one who matched the description of Robbie. One guy sucked on a Bud at the end of the bar as he fingered his cell phone and watched the doorway. I waited another five minutes before walking in.

He watched me, but had no reaction. When he realized that I was the one he was waiting for, anger flushed across his face as he stood up.

"You Munchian?" he asked.

"Who wants to know?"

"Don't be a wise guy. I ain't in the mood."

"Well, you don't look like the guy I'm supposed to meet."

"So what should he look like?"

"Who's asking?"

"You don't know who you're messin' with."

I told him I had a pretty good idea, and we stood there staring at each other. I knew he was trying to figure out what to do next. He then laughed and sat down.

"Okay, I'm Bo. You looking for Robbie?"

"I have an appointment with him. Where is he?"

"He's the boss. Don't gotta do nothing he don't wanna do. He sent me. Where's the Suburban?"

"It's around. Where's the money?"

"It's around. Did Robbie tell you how this works?"

"He made suggestions."

"Suggestions! Who do you think you're talking to?"

Bo pushed his jacket up so I could see the butt of his gun tucked in the waistband of his jeans. I looked him straight in the eye and gave the right pocket of my jacket a pat.

Bo took a deep breath and said, "The way this works is you give me the keys and I check out the goods."

"Not this time." I pulled a sandwich bag of weed from my pocket and tucked it into his hand. "Check it out. If Robbie likes it, I'll take you to it and we'll make the exchange." We shook hands, and Bo walked out the door.

Near Detroit

April 1996

I finally met Robbie on my third trip to Detroit, but I had a bad feeling about him. His greasy fingers and calloused hands told me he spent most of his time working on cars. We met at Walt's Coney Island. Robbie had a Coney dog, and I had a Coke. I was anxious to get this meeting over with.

"Okay, tell me how this works," I said as I tried to get down to business.

"Well, let me get this straight. You running Rizzo's loads for free?"

"To clear a debt with him."

"Bo says if you're smart, you could set up your own gig – sniff out a few good customers. I can set you up with suppliers. Boom. You're in. Stay away from Carlos and Rizzo. Nothing but trouble."

"So what are you saying?"

"Untie yourself from Rizzo. He's dumb. He lets Bo take advantage of him, getting half on the load. He got clocked by Carlos, leaving a brass indentation in his face. He's slow and fat."

"You planned on jacking my load, didn't you? Do I read that right?"

"Cars get stolen in Detroit. Rizzo tells me he's got a new guy coming. I ain't too pleased with his guys. Bo tells me I gotta meet you, a fearless Armenian who can run circles around him."

"So how do things work here?"

"You gotta move good product fast. Rizzo has a good supplier, but he's sloppy. I handle mostly west side – affluent whites, auto execs, and some blacks. Simon B., my east-side guy, deals with blacks really well but needs help with the Chaldean community. I've been trying to tap into his network in the southeast suburbs. If you get a rep delivering good stuff and delivering it fast, you'll do good. No shootings or jackings at our level. We just buy it and distribute it."

I walked him out to his Maserati. He reached in and pulled out a large envelope. I gave it a quick count when he handed it to me. There were ten half-inch stacks of hundred-dollar bills: $100,000.

"This your last freebie for Rizzo?"

"Maybe."

"You got my digits when you break free of him."

Phoenix, Arizona
September 1996

Now I needed two things: an additional supplier and a driver I could trust. I squared with Rizzo and told him I wanted to break ties with him. I was going to get back in the game, but on my own terms.

Bo had set me up with a connection in Detroit who regularly

wanted product. I pulled some connections together from LA and reconnected with Chico. I was making regular trips back to Cali to pick up product, which helped my reputation grow as a guy who could get quality product fast and efficiently – just like before, only now I was moving serious weight.

I pulled my Mercedes 500 SEL into the short driveway. I hadn't been there since the days of Roger Rabbit. Now I sat on fresh leather, purchased in a cash deal at Scottsdale Benz. The rickety front door of the house opened, and Nufo, not sure who was in his driveway, stepped out with a gun in his hand. I got out, leaned over the door, and said, "Nufo, man, it's me!"

Nufo was in a state of shock as he sat in the passenger seat playing with every electronic gadget within reach. My new ride and new threads stunned him. I had only told him that I had an opportunity for him and that he should pack a bag and be ready to head out for a few days. On the way to the airport, I explained the trips I'd been making to Detroit, the connections I'd made, and the serious weight I had moved – up to eight hundred pounds of weed a month.

I valet-parked the Benz, and we were soon sitting in the American Airlines luxury lounge discussing business. "We're heading to LA. I'll introduce you to my connection there, and then we'll run a load together to Detroit. You watch. First two trips, I'll be there. Then you can run the trips by yourself."

I could tell Nufo was impressed. He seemed to like the threads and the ride.

"I'll pay you $5,000 per load. Two runs a month should set you up pretty good. I buy directly from my supplier and move it myself. It's hard to trust anyone in this business, Nufo. I'm going to roll the dice and trust you, but if you get ripped off, consequences can be fatal. Watch and see how I do it; then do it exactly like me, and you should be golden. You okay with these terms?"

Nufo was all in. He had never made money like that before. It was a home boy's dream come true. We flew to LAX, and I introduced him to Chico, who ran an auto parts store outside East LA. I walked into the garage, grabbed the keys from a rack, and headed to a maroon Mountaineer. I popped the hatch to show Nufo how the product was hidden inside the speaker boxes.

"We've got two hundred and fifty pounds of skunk weed loaded here that we'll move. You ready?"

Of course, Nufo was excited. We stayed in a five-star hotel on the beach that night, and at five sharp the next morning, we were on our way to Detroit – and Nufo was on his way to becoming a loyal employee.

Phoenix, Arizona
December 1996

I was finally going to meet Big Mama Su. Lazy Su's Fish & Chips was on the southeast corner of Seventh Street and Portland, along with taco stands, thrift stores, and "Payday Loans." The filthy windows held cardboard signs with the day's specials. When I walked in, I saw Su's brother, AB, at the counter partaking of a greasy basket of breaded fish and French fries. AB and I met some time ago at a high-end VIP nightclub in town. I had heard that AB was well connected, and I learned that his prime connection was his sister, Su.

As I approached AB, I felt the grease under my shoes. When I noticed the greasy smears on the vinyl of the seat next to him, I decided to stand.

"Su!" he yelled.

The swinging double doors from the kitchen parted, and Su's enormous frame filled the entire doorway.

AB said, "Big Mama, this is the guy I was telling you about – Roger."

We shook hands, and then she said, "He's cute. Can I keep him?"

Then I saw a big dude come in through the side entrance. I instinctively slid my hand over my gun. He was wearing a T-shirt with Lazy Su's logo.

"You look sharp, Roger," Su said. "Too sharp for around here."

"I dress my part."

"Hey, Lazy Su," the dude shouted, "did that fool come through yet with my money?"

"Nothing yet, Mo, but I got people working on it."

"Hey, I need my money. I'm out nearly ten grand. I don't care how I get it."

"Mo," Su said, "I'm conducting business here."

Mo left, but I could see him through the window as he yanked the delivery sign off his car and ripped his shirt off. He climbed in and peeled off.

Su offered Mo's assistance if I needed a driver, but I really only trusted Nufo. I knew I could control him, and he was dependable.

Lazy Su showed me some samples of her product, and I liked it. We discussed the terms and negotiated a deal. I had a new supplier in Arizona now.

Tucson

February 1997

I got a frantic phone call from Rizzo. He was in trouble. "Carlos is gonna put a bullet between my eyes! Please help me!"

Rizzo told me that Robbie stiffed him on several loads. I didn't like to do business like that. Get stiffed once, blow out the knee cap; twice, silence him permanently. But Rizzo was an idiot, and now he owed Carlos more than $200,000. I asked him if he had the money.

"Yeah, I got it, and I made arrangements to pay him off, but he don't want me no more. He's gonna pop me after I pay him – I just know it."

I told him I couldn't do anything about it, and as usual, Rizzo had an idea. "I need someone with irons. Even if you just sit in the background, just be there to let him know he's in trouble if he tries anything. I'll get in, pay up, and get out real quick. I'll pay you well to be my back up; otherwise, he'll kill me."

I drove down I-10 toward Tucson in my Mercedes 600 Coup with bulletproof glass. My vanity plate read "Hrach." I was moving much more weight, and the Chaldean cartel did not play games. Things were going great, and I felt untouchable. Nothing was going to stop me. Nothing.

I pulled into the driveway and parked next to Carlos's black Crown Vic. I reached under the front seat and grabbed my Colt .45 and the leather pouch with the money. I opened the screen, knocked, and then pushed the door open – fast. Carlos was shouting, and Rizzo was whimpering, so they didn't hear me. I saw them in the kitchen. Carlos had a gun barrel stuck to Rizzo's temple while he was pleading for his life.

"I told you, Carlos. I ain't got it here, but it's coming. I promise."

I put my thumb on the Colt's hammer and said, "Put the gun down, Carlos, nice and slow." I stepped into the kitchen and fixed my gunsight between his eyes.

"What are you doing here? This is between me and him."

I pulled the cash out and dropped it on the table. "I'm here to broker a peace settlement. Take your cash and get out. That's all you gotta do."

He picked it up and did a first count. Then he counted it again. "One hundred and eighty thousand. Stupid, you're twenty grand short."

"Two hundred thousand minus my 10 percent."

Carlos asked, "Ten percent? For what?"

"I warned you. I only tell you once." Then I proceeded to work him over, slamming his head to the table and then to the floor. I grabbed the wad of cash and shoved it in his mouth, using the barrel of my Colt to wedge it in. I yanked him to his feet and bounced him against the wall before I tossed him through the screen door.

He collapsed on the front porch, so I shoved him toward his car. "Nice doing business with you, Carlos."

Rizzo was soaking wet with sweat when I returned to the kitchen. He said, "I think I need a new connection. Can you set me up?"

"I'll see what I can do. I'm done working for free, Rizzo. My debt to you has been paid in full. I didn't even get a thank you for saving your life today."

Chapter 8

The Accident

Sevier County, Utah
April 1997

Nufo had been working out well after we made that agreement over the Big Mac. I could trust him with delivery to Detroit. He was faithful to me, and I needed that.

I had customers all over who kept me hopping nonstop, so it was important for me to be able to trust my driver. I managed to stay one step ahead of the law by always keeping a low profile and paying high-dollar lawyers for advice on the best way to commit a crime. I even got married to create a clean image. The wedding was a big deal. My parents threw a huge Armenian gig, but I soon realized that married life was not for me. I contacted my attorney and started divorce proceedings to close the marriage out in an annulment as quickly as possible. It was just another business transaction to me.

I made fast connections, which involved regular trips to Mexico. I had to check out dope farms to make sure the product was quality and that delivery routes were clear. Lots had changed from the old days. The busier I got with the business, the less I used. No more red eyes from using my own supply. I dressed sharp and reinvested my dough. I felt unstoppable.

Nufo never managed to quit the dope. The more money he made, the more he used. I warned him about his smoking habit during runs, but he was still the only person I trusted to make the runs. I tried to be generous with Nufo and always paid him well and on time to keep him happy. I gave him a bonus when he recruited a new driver, his adopted father, whom everyone called Pops. I bought him a new ride, a white Suburban, to pick up a small load in LA. This shipment was going to a new connection in Denver by his regular route, I-15 out of California, through Utah to the I-70 split and into Denver. Nufo had been making runs without any trouble until one particular day.

He exited I-15 and headed east on I-70, staying within the speed limit. He told me that when I-70 curved northeast outside of Sevier, he got uncomfortable because of the number of police cruisers that were passing him. That was a bad omen. At the city of Joseph, he decided to get off the freeway and take State Route 118. That was not a wise decision. I had taught him better. I told him to always stick to the interstates because he'd look more suspicious if he was pulled over on a back road with out-of-state plates. I had given him a cover story if that happened on the interstate, but on the back roads, the story didn't always stack up. They always want to check you out a little more.

State Route 118 became Route 120 just past the Richfield Municipal Airport, and it turned into Main Street through the little town of Richfield. Five miles out of town, Nufo saw brake lights ahead and a long line of traffic. After ten minutes of crawling along, he saw the blue lights of sheriff cars ahead. Three of them. The deputies were stopping each passing car, asking a question. If they answered right, they were waved through. If they answered wrong, they had to pull over for more questions.

Nufo said he considered splitting off and heading south like some cars behind him had. He knew he could go another way, but he'd lose time. He hadn't seen any K-9s around, and the deputy seemed to be waving cars through. I had told Nufo to always wear a shirt and tie and act confident. He had followed all of my advice. He cracked the windows to make sure the Suburban was aired out.

Now it was his turn. He rolled down the window. The deputy leaned down and said, "Afternoon, sir."

"Afternoon, officer."

"Where are you driving from?"

"Arizona. Phoenix area."

"Where you headed?"

"Denver."

"For what?"

At that point, Nufo started getting nervous. This was more than the one question the deputy had asked the other drivers.

"Business. It's part of my route."

"What kind of business?"

"Tools mostly." I had prepared Nufo for this with information on a dummy corporation in the construction supply business. He showed the deputy a glossy brochure of power tools. "National sales rep. I cover the entire United States."

"I'm smelling something in your vehicle that doesn't smell like tool oil. I'd say if I popped open the back, we'd find a few bales of dope."

"Okay, I'll bet you the five hundred bucks in my wallet that you're wrong."

"You want to pull off to the side over there for me, sir?"

Nufo knew he had made a mistake.

I really did not need or want this. Not now. Nufo called around midnight. I guess they wouldn't let him call sooner. In the Seveir County lockup, they wanted him to either give up his source or face hard time.

"Roger, they're talking class 2 felonies. Four of them. Fifteen years a pop. They say they're going to bring in the Feds and make an example of me."

I knew he was being recorded and was thankful he was being careful of what he said. This was standard business, but I had coached Nufo and Pops in what to expect and how to handle things. I told

them to always stay calm and then call me right away. Well, Nufo
had called, but he sure didn't sound calm.

"What's your bail?"

"Thirty grand! Can you believe it?"

"Jay will take care of it. You should be out in forty-eight hours."

Jay Andrews was my retained attorney, one of the best. "Then stay
calm. Remember your rights. Don't tell them anything without an
attorney. You can remember that, can't you?"

"Yeah, Roger, but it's freaking me out."

The timing of this was not good. I was busy dealing with supply
issues, crazy customers, and trying to hang on to the business. I was
still trying to get this divorce finalized. What a stupid mistake it was
to get married to look clean and keep my parents happy! I knew I
didn't want to settle down. It was like a prison. I couldn't wait until
Jay had the papers drawn up and I could be free – back in the fast lane.

Business was growing large and moving fast, but never fast enough
to satisfy my lust for more. More money. More women. More power.

A future free of entanglements, with me in control, was just
waiting for me. It promised the erasure of the past – the immigrant
boy who spoke little English and wore the same clothes every day. I
had been afraid with low self-esteem, but that image was fading as
I acquired money and power. The faster I pushed, the faster that old
lowlife disappeared. I was Hrach Roger Munchian, a man of infinite
wealth and power.

But when Nufo called, I had to put everything else aside and place
that call to Jay, which I really did not want to do. I knew we had to
get Nufo out of there before he spilled his guts. I had too much at
stake. I had too much to lose.

Sevier County Jail
July 1997
The metal door to the pod rolled open, and reeking hot air rushed in.
All was quiet with the inmates in their cells on lockdown. Wearing

his striped suit, courtesy of the Sevier County Sheriff's Office, Nufo stepped over the threshold into the pod.

The officer followed him up a flight of stairs and down a catwalk with a metal rail and jail cells. One door rolled open – Jail pod C, Cell 18. That would be Nufo's new home for the next three months. The cell door slammed shut as he stared at the metal sink, the stainless-steel toilet, and the thin mattress on the metal slab.

I had given his loads to Pops for the time being. I told Nufo that he could survive. He only had to serve three months. His release date was October 20, 1997, and he was counting down the days. He was sure that he'd be back at it on October 21, 1997.

What he didn't know, though, was that by that time, things were going to be different. I didn't know that either.

Sky Harbor Airport
August 1997

I pulled up to the curb and told Karine to get out. She looked dumbfounded and shocked as she stood there with the plane ticket that I bought her, a one-way, all-expenses-paid trip to Burbank, California.

"Jay filed the divorce papers this morning. You'll get your copy in the mail. Be sure to get them notarized when you sign. Bye, Karine. Sorry it didn't work out."

"But what about the baby? Your child?"

"Karine, there is no child. You miscarried."

"But my pregnancy was a sign that God wants to bring us children. You can't do this."

"Don't bring God into this. God's got nothing to do with my life. I run my own show. God can sit by and watch if He wants. It's over, Karine."

I knew that Karine loved my lifestyle, wealth, and possessions. Of course, she had no idea where the money came from. The wedding had included vows, but what was that all about? They were just words. In reality, marriage to me was just a simple business transaction. It was nothing but a contract. Yes, a deal was a deal, but a deal could be broken with the right lawyer.

As I pulled away from the curb, I looked in the rearview mirror and saw her. She was standing there with a look of disbelief while the baggage guy loaded her luggage onto the cart. I headed up State Road 51, northbound from the airport, clocking 120 mph. It wasn't fast enough. I pushed the accelerator down and pushed the Porsche to its limit. I wanted to get away as fast as I could. Fast felt good. Faster and faster, but even faster wasn't enough.

No. Nothing was fast enough, so I pushed harder. God could sit by and watch.

Phoenix
September 25, 1997
12:58 a.m.

A month later I floored the accelerator of my Mercedes-Benz S 600 Coupe. The dotted center line on eastbound I-10 blurred into solid white, and the speedometer approached its upper limits. My new girl, Alma, sank back into her seat at the rapid acceleration, but her warm hand lingered on my leg.

I looked at Benny and Maria in the rearview mirror. Blood had drained from Benny's face, and his Heineken had soaked his shirt. "Don't you dare lose it back there, man. If you puke in here, you're forking it over to get this car detailed."

With another glimpse in the mirror, I saw Maria's dainty, polished fingers caress Benny's cheek. I lost sight of him as I savored the moment. The world was flashing by in a vodka-induced flurry, and I was reveling in my freedom and power. Streetlights streamed overhead like a laser, and exit signs flew by in a green swirl.

Alma curled up close to me, and my heart raced as I glanced at her. I felt the warmth of her body and inhaled the scent of her perfume. I caught a hint of alcohol as she nuzzled into my neck. I wanted to get home fast. I floored the accelerator again, and the speedometer made it to about 130 mph.

Like all the women in my life, Alma wanted more out of our relationship. I liked her, maybe even more than the others, but I was unbridled and I liked it that way. My life was fast-paced and full of carnal revelry of new conquests – the conquest of another deal, another chick, another million. I would make it and make it fast. There was no slowing down.

Suddenly Benny screamed, "Slow down!" I took my eyes off Alma's legs and saw the taillights of a semi racing toward us. I cranked the wheel left. My right bumper was just inches from grazing the trailer. I looked in the rearview mirror and saw the truck's headlights fade fast. Then I saw Benny take another swig of Heineken. Maria seemed clueless as to what had just happened. I didn't know Benny well. He was a dimpled crowd-pleaser who was one of the regulars at the Empire Night Club VIP Lounge. He'd been drawn to my generosity and had made a move on Maria that night.

To the Empire Night Club management, these regulars were valued customers. To me, this was my village with my people. We had our own special section at the club – the Lounge. We always had an ebb and flow of strangers and vagabonds, but the core group gave me a sense of belonging, a sense of meaning, a sense of purpose. I took care of them. They were my family. I flashed the green, plastic-coated platinum card. I kept the bar taps primed and the pour spouts pouring. I spent very little time alone. My money drew friends and lots of hot chicks. Money secured an unscathed time in an indifferent world for me. I thought I had everything I needed, and hooking up Benny with Maria was just one more pious act of service that added meaning to my life.

I floored it again and watched the road rush by. A glimpse in the mirror produced a perfect picture of my past: a fast-flying world of luxury. It felt good. It felt right.

I want it all. I want everything. God can sit by and watch.

I saw mile marker 148 ahead, and I knew we were within two miles of our exit. It was coming fast. Adrenaline and alcohol drove me on. The road narrowed in the vodka haze as Alma whispered in my ear, but suddenly a mist of rain distorted the road. It was only a light sprinkle, but at my speed, the droplets were driven into the windshield in a pelting, battering fashion. The bright dash lights illuminated the speedometer to a fuzzy 130 mph as Exit 150 rushed toward us. I saw the yellow sign that indicated a sharp curve ahead and warned drivers to slow down to 45 mph. I slowed down only to compensate a little for the wet conditions, but anything under 100 mph made me feel as if my past would catch up with me. I had that euphoric vigor that made me feel invincible.

I felt it in my hands and body before my brain engaged enough to know that something had gone terribly wrong. The steering wheel shook, the rear end fishtailed counterclockwise, and the tires bounced and squealed. The smell of burning rubber seeped up through the wheel wells and into the car.

Suddenly everyone was silent in the car. My shoulder harness sucked me deep into my seat, and even my cry of alarm was shut off. I hung on as tightly as I could, but the steering wheel was ripped from my grip as we hit the curve. I heard the crunch of metal and I felt the floor buckle. My knees slammed into the steering column as the curb gutted the car's underside and sent us airborne. My head snapped forward, choking off my cries from the white-hot pain in my knees. The car landed in the gravel with an unstoppable force and slid sideways through the gore point where I-10 ended and northbound I-17 began. It then skidded across three lanes and shredded rubber as it stormed toward the cement barrier wall.

My ears ached from the sound of the tires squealing on cement, and my nose burned from the stench of the rubber. I saw Benny's face, ashen white with horror, as we contacted the wall. The fender buckled on impact. The crushed hood rose through the smoke-like volcanic flurry of glass, metal shards, and debris. The window shattered, and Benny's face was speckled in blood.

I remember hearing Alma scream and seeing the passenger side airbag shoot out from the dash, swallowing her whole. The car, however, continued to tumble along the wall, creating a shower of sparks that lit the interior in a blaze of fiery incandescence. The car was demolishing itself as it skidded and flipped with a force that sucked me deeper into the leather seat. How I wanted to go back in time as I spun with the car!

How far back could I go? Moments ago, when the rain hit as a warning to slow down? Back to the Empire Night Club? Back to my first hit of dope?

How does one have so many thoughts in such a short space of time? However, as I considered each thought, I knew there was no hope. It would not help to go back. I knew we were all going to die that night, at that very moment. I knew I had killed them all.

My bulletproof windshield had splintered, and it turned to powder in the next impact with the wall. I watched my world spin through that distorted view, like snapshots, like a child's toy, like a broken View-Master. I heard a scream as a fragile life was sucked from the car. I saw a twisted, disjointed figure fly past that passenger window.

It can't be real. It can't be her.

The China-doll duplicate of Alma turned over in mid-flight, staring at me in frozen, anguished shock. I fought the force that cemented my hands to the wheel and tried to reach her. I felt the car ricochet off the wall and go wheels up in a rolling tumble. My airbag deployed, and I couldn't breathe. I couldn't see. My head seemed to explode. Then my world went black.

Part 2

God Restores

Chapter 9

My Damascus Road

Phoenix
September 25, 1997
1:33 a.m.

That whole ride, including the accident, only took about thirty-five minutes. I am told that while I was blacked out, a Honda Accord stopped in the middle of the exit ramp. A young couple, Jenny and Jason, had seen the wreckage. Jason saw the victims.

"There's bodies! Bodies!" he yelled.

At first, the car behind them laid on the horn, but then the four-way blinkers came on. The doors popped open and two guys rushed to the guardrail to get a better look.

"Oh, man, I gotta check this out," Jason said as he jumped out.

They had been drinking at a frat party and were on their way home. Jenny didn't want to talk to cops with alcohol on her breath. "Come on, Jason, let's get out of here."

"Hey, maybe you should, like, call 9-1-1 or something."

"We'll get busted. Come on, Jason."

"Where we gonna go? The road's totally blocked with bodies and stuff."

When Jenny heard the bloodcurdling scream, she got out and

joined the others at the guardrail. She saw the dead girls and heard Benny on his phone. He had been walking around as he made a frantic call. Suddenly he hopped the barrier wall and slid down the embankment. A white Pathfinder came to a screeching halt on the road below. Benny jumped into the back, and the truck took off, squealing its tires as it sped away.

Jenny heard sirens in the distance, and she knew they would have to talk to the cops. She asked, "Got any mints, Jason?"

My world had not gone black for very long. Guilt broke through that blackness and jolted me back to reality. After I extricated myself from the car and saw what I had done, I wanted to end my life quickly with a bullet from my own gun. First, I wrote a note identifying myself. Then I searched for the gun. It should have been under the seat, but I couldn't find it. In my frantic search for the weapon that was no longer there, I only gashed my hands by rubbing them through the shattered glass that covered the floorboards. I looked up and saw the bridge. I would jump. I would end this nightmare in one leap, but I had to hurry.

The police closed in fast. Officer Ken Rossie, driving K-9 Unit 021, stepped on his accelerator and hit his lights when he spotted me racing across the street as I was heading for the railing of the Salt River Bridge. He had already responded to a call about an individual who had fled the scene. The Firebird helicopter circled overhead and spotted me limping and stumbling toward the railing. I was in plain sight. Since the ravine floor was a four-story drop, he called it a suicide risk and shouted into his mic, "Police! Stay where you are!"

I heard the other units coming up fast, but I was sure I could make it and end this nightmare. Officer Rossie realized he could not get to me quickly enough, so he hit the brakes, fishtailed the cruiser, and flipped the switch to the K-9 Door Popper. The rear door flew open, and Digger darted out of the car. Rossie whipped open his door and sprinted toward me, shouting into his mic to alert the responding units: "K-9 released! Suspect going over the rail!"

My heart sank when I heard that, but adrenaline rushed through my body. Police spotlights turned the night into day as I made my limping dash. Digger grabbed the leg of my pants, but I broke free from his fangs. That momentum sent me to the rail. I felt my legs fly into the air, and I saw the sharp rocks and foliage below. It was over.

God, help me! God, help me!

My plunge ended abruptly as the growl of the beast filled the air again. I heard my own anguished cries from my failure to end my life. I tumbled to the sidewalk, looked up, and saw the gnarling teeth of the German shepherd as it whipped its head back and forth with saliva flying from its vice-grip jowls.

Black shoes raced toward me, and I heard shouts and orders warning me not to move. Arms restrained me and hurled me down as I reached for the rail. Sidewalk grit dug into my cheek. Then I felt the familiar metallic clank of the cold metal surrounding my wrists. The handcuffs were tight, painfully denying the flow of blood to my fingertips.

The blinding police light burned white hot inside my head as the police asked me questions – questions that I didn't understand and couldn't hear well in the midst of the confusion of the snarling dog, overhead copter, and radio chatter. I was yanked to my feet. The mix of tears and bright lights blinded me, but I was shoved against the police cruiser. I winced at the pain from a kick to the ankles to force me to spread my legs. Then more commands and more questions – questions about the car, the wreck, and the victims.

After slamming my head into the hood of the cruiser, the officer angrily said, "They're dead! How does it feel? How does it feel to have taken two innocent lives?" I was slammed twice more against the door. "Get in the car, you bonehead!"

The door slammed shut, and I peered through the mesh caging at another officer. I knew I would be looking at the world like this for a very long time, with things distorted behind bars and caging.

The cop drove slowly past the wreckage to force me one last time to see the damage I'd caused. As we passed, I saw the gold-framed vanity plate on the bumper of the wreckage, distorted by my tears: HRACH.

Who's Hrach, anyway? Who are you now, Hrach? Who are you now? God, help me.

When we got to the Madison Street Jail a couple hours later, I was dragged down, hog-tied, and taken into the horseshoe-shaped intake area. Suddenly a spasm hit my gut. I turned, bent, and twisted over. I broke free from the grips of the two detention officers, fell on the floor, and retched. Bile poured uncontrollably from my stomach. I saw visions of the accident scene over and over. The *HRACH* vanity plate mocked me from the wreckage. I saw a bundle of bloody clothing – Alma's sequin dress next to the paramedics who were working on her half-naked body, trying to restore her life.

The detention officers ended my retches by slamming me into a cinder-block wall and yanking me down by my hair. Pain overpowered me so much that it cut off my cries of anguish and rage. They tightened my handcuffs to the max, almost cutting off the blood flow. They then yanked my joints to the point of dislocation and carried me, hog-tied, down the horseshoe hallway. My anger exploded into an unbridled rage that intensified my fight. I was teetering on the verge of insanity – spitting, biting, and kicking at the officers. For my safety and theirs, they strapped me into the black "crazy" chair on wheels and put a facemask over me. The pain brought me close to unconsciousness. I fought the restraints, but the straps gave only an inch and cut deeply into my arms and legs when I resisted. Threats and obscenities poured out of my mouth and echoed off the intake walls of the horseshoe.

All my fussing prompted whoops and hollers from the holding tanks as others were egging me on – this spoiled brat all dressed in his Armani clothes not wanting to get into his striped jammies.

"Let me out of this thing," I screamed.

The pain from my shattered knee and torn ligament surged as rage forced my legs to tremble. As I fought the restraints, I felt the darkness of an inhuman abyss rise from the depths of hell. Power and control were gone. I was helplessly engulfed in an eternal anguish with no escape.

I was in the belly of the whale with no way out. Nothing could rescue me, not even the gods I'd served so faithfully – the gods of sex, drugs, money, and power. They were not to be found in this pit of hopelessness.

All my gods had abandoned me. I was now eternally alone with the one person I hated the most – my nemesis and archenemy – me, Hrach Roger Munchian, a.k.a. "Roger Rabbit." I hated him more than death itself.

"God," I heard my voice call out. Blood pounded in my head, pumped by a grieving heart. "Are You there, God? Are You there?" I screamed until I tasted blood in my throat. I fell back into the chair as fatigue overcame me. For the first time in my life, I wondered if God was real. Did He actually exist? Until that point, the only god I believed in and trusted with my life was a god called Money.

"God!" I cried again. My chest trembled. The pain from my cracked ribs and bruised muscles caused convulsive gasping as I screamed out to God. I sobbed uncontrollably. Tears washed my cheeks and burned the gashes that disfigured my face. Unbearable guilt tormented me as I fought the reality of what I had done. The nightmare continually flashed in my mind, including Alma lying on the blood-slick pavement, cold and lifeless. I knew that nothing in my control could undo this.

Roger Munchian was nothing more than a murderer, a caged monster, soon to be disposed of by the justice system. My sobs echoed remorsefully throughout the entire jailhouse.

I cried out, "God, if You're there, God, help me! Oh, please help me!"

The god of money that I'd worshipped all my life couldn't help me. All my wealth couldn't get me out of this mess. For the first time ever, no bail was available, and I wasn't bondable.

"I'm without hope. I'm at Your mercy, almighty God. Only You can do the miracles that my money and high-priced attorneys can no longer do. I never thought I needed You because I had too much money; but I need You now. Help me. Help me. Help me. Oh, God – help!"

Chapter 10

First Steps on the Damascus Road

Madison Street Jail
September 25, 1997
Early Dawn

The stench of urine, vomit, and bile greeted me as I woke in the early dawn. With a burning throat and stinking breath, I tried to pry my eyes open. My stomach still heaved and my head pounded.

The heavy clank of the cell door jarred my eyes wide open. Sometime during the night, I had been moved to the isolation cell across the hall from the "crazy" chair and had been chained to a ring embedded in the cement slab that was my bed. The approaching detention officer was a blur. He was saying something. His mouth was moving, but the words were garbled like a scrambled message. "Lucked out . . . come out. We have to rebook you through intake . . . lucky SOB. Let go, man!"

He was trying to take something from me, something that was in my hand. I held tight. It must be something important. Then the detention officer tried to talk to me again. "Just let go, man! Okay, fine; you want the old one, fine."

Finally, my eyes focused. The detention officer had grabbed the old intake paperwork that I had clung to all night – the papers that charged me with two counts of manslaughter and a DUI, the ones they had handed to me at intake that officially declared I was drunk and a murderer. I let go and took the new set of papers that the officer was handing to me.

"You sure lucked out on this one. Never seen nothing like this before in all my years working at this zoo."

I sat up and looked at the new papers. With my head throbbing and on the verge of exploding, I could finally focus on the words.

Maricopa County Sheriff's Office

Intake, Madison

Inmate: P443221, Munchian, Hrach "Roger."

Charges: Count 1, Aggravated Assault with a Deadly Weapon.

Count 2, Aggravated Assault with a Deadly Weapon.

Count 1, Driving under the Influence of Alcohol.

The door slammed shut. Through the thick Plexiglas window, I watched the officer walk away from my concrete cage with my old intake papers.

Assault? What's going on?

I remembered my desperate pleas from the night before. In fact, I could almost hear them echoing off the cement walls and coming back to me. *God, help me!*

I had to wonder if God had heard me. I suddenly felt a comfort unlike anything I had ever felt before, as if I heard God answer, "*I heard you. Trust Me, Roger. Call out to Me, and I will show you great and wonderful things. Trust Me.*"

Only later would I realize that this was my Damascus Road experience (see Acts 9). I was at the end of myself and my gods. I had to wonder if God was actually real. Was He not just sitting on the side without a care? Did He really care about me?

It wasn't until I had been processed out of jail that I found out what happened. As I waited for bail, I called Jay, my Arizona attorney. He kept asking me what I was talking about. What manslaughter charges? "Your charges are two counts of aggravated assault and a DUI, Roger. The victims are alive. In critical condition, but alive."

"Jay, that's impossible! They were dead!" I could still hear the cop's words in my head: *They're dead. How does it feel to have taken two innocent lives?*

"I don't have the full hospital report yet, Roger, but you're booked on two counts of aggravated assault, class 2 felonies, and a DUI. That means they found signs of life in the victims. They could be completely brain dead from now until the end of your days, and it ain't changing to manslaughter. Don't get me wrong. These are very serious charges."

"They were dead, Jay."

"Let's get your bail settled, and we can talk in the office."

"You should have seen them, Jay! There's no way they were alive."

Bail was $20,000, but I was out by noon, as usual, and sitting in Jay's office.

"You look horrible, all banged up like that, but we can beat this thing."

"I shouldn't even be alive. None of us should."

Jay just sat at his desk sifting through my open file. When I winced from the pain in my knee, he looked up and said, "You really should get that looked at."

"What do you mean critical condition, Jay?"

"Comas. Both of them."

God, help me! I know they were dead.

"I heard you. Trust Me. I will show you great and wonderful things."

"In the tank, Jay. Down at Madison. I woke up, and they took my papers. Manslaughter. That's what they booked me for initially."

Jay shuffled through my file again and shook his head. "Look, Roger, this is a tight case. Aggravated assault is a class 2 felony. We're looking at ten years minimum per count. That's twenty long. If one of them doesn't make it, we add manslaughter to that. If neither makes it, we're potentially facing a capital case."

Death row didn't faze me. I wanted to be dead anyway, but I kept hearing a voice: *"Trust Me. I have great plans for you."*

If you're real, God, help me. Help me!

"I'm here."

Who are you?

"I'm Jesus. I'm not just standing by watching. I'm with you. Always."

Jay continued to shuffle papers and talk about my defense. "We'll make an attempt at reasonable doubt that you were driving the vehicle. If anyone can beat this thing, I can."

I felt sick the way Jay stared at the file, business as usual. I was tired, confused, and ashamed. I went home and slept for two days straight. I woke up on Saturday morning, still dazed, but Alma was on my mind. I had to see her. I had to see for myself.

St. Joseph's Hospital
Phoenix
September 29, 1997

Leaning hard on my crutch, I hobbled down the hall of the intensive care unit. My knee had been shattered and my ligaments had been shredded in the accident. My doctor had recommended immediate surgery, but I had other things to do first.

Alma was in room 2231. I stood outside the door and stared through the little window. My heart broke to see her delicate body hooked up to tubes and wires. Fluids ran in and out of her. Her chest heaved in short, labored breaths, thanks to the ventilator. The lips that were once full of life and laughter were now dry and chapped.

I tasted the salt from my tears that flooded past my lips. I pushed the door open and hobbled to her bedside to see up close what I had done. I listened to the gurgle in her throat with every breath while the blip on the screen next to her bed recorded signs of life. Looking at this broken child of God, I could see the intricacies of the handiwork of God.

What have I done? Oh, God, what have I done to Your beautiful creation?

Yet I had an inexplicable peace beneath my anguish. God was fixing her. Only God could fix what I had destroyed. How many other lives had I destroyed? Could God heal them too?

I stayed until they kicked me out, and then I sat in my Porsche in the hospital garage. I stared at my pager and realized I had missed calls demanding shipment statuses, pickups, and urgent needs for product. I also missed calls from Jay and Rizzo.

I chose to ignore them and drive over to Rainbow Body and Repair where Jay had arranged for the Mercedes to be towed. I stepped out of the Porsche with its new-car smell to get a better view of the Mercedes. Sitting under the dim light of the garage, the crumpled mass that had been the Mercedes looked less deadly than it had at the manslaughter scene. It had been searched, probed, photographed, measured, and scrutinized. It was evidence, a weapon, a death trap. Now in the greasy morgue, it was junk. It had a pulverized windshield, buckled wheel wells, and a crumpled hood. The oily death stench of the Mercedes mixed with the oaky new-car aroma pouring from the Porsche and made me realize that both scents were the same: emptiness, nothingness, meaninglessness.

Why am I still here? Talk to me, God. Help me find You. Oh, please help! Show me the truth, God!

"Trust Me, Roger. I have a plan for you. Just trust Me. Watch what I am going to do."

Just as in my younger days in the projects of Los Angeles, I decided to chase what I wanted; so instead of pursuing money and sex this time, I pursued God by researching the most popular faith foundations. I wanted facts. I started to research science and history because I did not trust any human opinion, traditions, or schools of thought.

I also wanted to check out a church, and that's how I met Pastor Frank. I had started a car dealership, Rainbow Auto Sales, as a front for my money laundering several years prior to this. I had connected with some shady guys in the world of partying – DeSoto and his brothers – who ran another dealership. One of the brothers branched off and offered to operate my dealership as a manager. When Rainbow Auto Sales opened up, Pastor Frank would come around and hang out because he knew these guys. He shared the message and planted seeds. Frank knew the family, and the family was involved in his little church. When all of this happened with the accident, somehow someone referred me to him. So we had originally connected on the dealership yard before the accident, but I never thought much about him; he was just there. He would sometimes show up when I happened to be there. After the accident, though, I was searching. I needed answers about God.

Sevier County, Utah
October 20, 1997

I watched Nufo come through the doors of the Sevier County Jail. Without having seen much sunlight during his three months there, his brown skin was much paler than when he entered. He hopped into the Porsche and let out a howl. "Ah, fresh air at last!"

I released the clutch and made tracks out of the parking lot. I pushed the needle past ninety as we raced south on State Route 15. Nufo looked at the speedometer.

"Man, Rog, ninety is grandma speed for this piece of machinery. Punch it, man. I wanna get out of this state as fast as possible."

I held it at ninety and sensed Nufo staring at my knee. "I take it you heard."

"Yeah. Pops, he told me about it. Said you had some legal troubles."

"I ain't worried about the legal stuff, Nufo. I took the lives of two girls."

"Pop said they didn't expire or nothin'. Said you was looking at doing ten large apiece for assault."

I didn't say anything at first. I just stared out the windshield and watched the desert fly by. Finally I said, "No, I killed them. God saved them. God saved me."

"What do you mean, Rog?"

"They were dead at the scene. You should have seen them. They strapped me in the crazy chair and locked me up."

"But Pops said . . ."

"I don't care what Pops said, Nufo! They were dead, and I was the button man!"

"*Were* dead?"

"You don't know what it's like. If I could have died in their place, I would have. For the first time in my life, I felt completely helpless. No matter how many millions I've made, no matter how much power I had – I couldn't fix it. It's like falling into a big black hole, an empty, cold, black hole where all you got is yourself – the one person you hate more than anything in the world. That's the guy I thought I was going to have to spend the rest of my life alone with."

"Man, Roger, you're freaking me out."

"I haven't told anyone yet, Nufo. No one but you. Down there in that hole, in the belly of that whale, there was only one glimmer of light. There was only one hope – God."

"Oh, man, have you gone religious on me? Oh, that's great! Just what we need."

"For the first time in my life, He was real. Everything was going to be okay if I asked Him. So I did. Nufo, I was holding my booking papers in my hands that said manslaughter. I tossed my guts so much that the papers were covered with bloody puke. I was so full of grief that I puked until I didn't have anything left to toss but blood."

"Grief or tequila. It's called the dry heaves, dude. Take a couple Tylenol and get over it."

"I called out to God for help, and they found life in the girls somewhere between the scene and the hospital. He rescued me by restoring their lives. I didn't get arrested that night – I got rescued. God rescued me!"

"You're giving me goosebumps, man."

"Maria came out of her coma a few weeks ago. Then a week ago, Alma came out too. It's got me thinking, you know, about all that we've been doing. I just don't think I can do this anymore."

"Hey, be careful now, Rog, okay? I mean, we got a good thing going here."

"Good thing, Nufo? Where have you been the last three months? Eating maggot-infested tapioca, wearing stripes, and sleeping with your head six inches from the toilet."

"It was only three months. County time ain't the best, but it's over. I survived and am ready to get back in the game."

I shook my head. "You ain't getting it. Our luck is running thin. I was looking at death row. Two counts of manslaughter and they fry you. Even if Jay could get me off, I just sense God's got something bigger, something better than this. He's got my attention now. He's calling me. He rescued me from myself."

"Calling you? He's God."

"I've been checking out a church, Nufo, and talking to Pastor Frank. He showed me a story in the Bible about a guy named Saul who was killing Christians."

"The Bible? Oh man, Rog, don't tell me you're one of those Bible thumpers now too?"

"Saul was on his way to Damascus and got knocked off his horse by a blinding light. Then he heard the voice of Jesus."

"Oh no. Not the 'J' word!"

"Shut up! God blinded Saul and knocked him down to get his attention. His name later became Paul. Pastor Frank says God had a plan for Paul's life. It was his Damascus moment. Funny. Saul's Damascus moment came at noon on an animal in the desert; mine came at dawn strapped to a chair in the Maricopa County hole."

"Seriously, Rog, don't go soft. We got a lot of bad people around us. We built something good, and there's guys who would kill to get a piece of it. If they sense you've gone weak, they'll pounce. You can't just walk away from this – not with all we've done."

"We, Nufo? We?"

"Sorry. They're your connections. It's yours. But you understand, don't you? If any of the punks we deal with decide you gotta go, you get popped in twenty minutes. If they think you're weak, you become a threat. They pop you, they pop me, and they take it over. We've seen it happen, man. I don't want to be a statistic, okay?"

I thought about it. Nufo was right. You just don't get out of this business without making people nervous. I knew more than a dozen homies and bangers who would pop me in a second if they thought they could hook into my suppliers. Rizzo was at the top of the list.

I also knew that God had something bigger – and better. I had recently read, *From the east I summon a bird of prey; from a far-off land, a man to fulfill my purpose. What I have said, that I will bring about; what I have planned, that I will do* (Isaiah 46:11).

God, is it me? Have you summoned me to fulfill Your purpose? Why pick me, God? After all I've done?

"Trust Me, Roger. Just trust Me."

Near St. Louis
March 1998
"I'm hungry," Nufo said, interrupting my thoughts. "McDonald's, next exit. Mind if I pull off?"

"Yeah, we got time."

"You hungry?"

"No, not really."

I didn't feel much like talking, and Nufo knew it. We were running a 250-pound load up from the Mexican border to Simen in Detroit. My thoughts had been on my last court case. It had been five months since the indictment. It made me wonder how God was going to get me out of this. I also wondered how I could get away from Rizzo. He was too reckless, even putting the entire ring of cartels in jeopardy. I knew it was only a matter of time before the moron sold to some narc, and then we'd all be getting measured for orange ADOC jump suits. I had connected Rizzo with Lazy Su and cut him loose as a customer, but I kept control of my connections.

Nufo exited the highway and pulled into the McDonald's drive-through. He ordered his usual Big Mac, extra-large fries, and a Coke. Then we got back on eastbound I-80.

"You know you haven't eaten since Amarillo," he said.

"I told you. I'm not hungry."

"You wanna know why you're losing so many customers?"

"Rizzo was no loss. He's a moron, and morons are dangerous."

"Okay, but look. You gotta dial the Jesus thing back a few clicks, okay? Listen, man, the Jesus talk was all over that hole in Sevier County. Guys are talking that salvation smack all the time. Bibles were all over the place. We had so many Bibles up there, they tore them up and used the pages to roll joints. They were tokin' God's Word. Guys who get thrown in the bucket turn religious real fast. They say they finally got Jesus, that Jesus is gonna help them turn it around. They say that Jesus is in their heart. One guy went preaching in the rec room all the time – right until he got released. Thirty days later, he was back in the hole. He's not saying much this time."

"What's your point, Nufo?"

"This Jesus stuff is making people nervous. It's okay if you get a little religious, but Jesus is Jesus, and business is business."

"But I've been studying and searching. I believe what I believe because I'm investigating this God who answered my cry for help. I need to know if He's real. I need to know if the Bible's true. Did you know that the guy who discovered currents in the sea found it in the

Bible first? Matthew Maury was a scientist who mapped the *paths of the sea* because he read about them in Psalm 8."

I sensed that I couldn't say anymore to Nufo, but I knew that what I found in history and science convinced me that the Bible was true, even though I still had issues with trusting people and their opinions about God. Facts were facts. The Bible and Jesus had more evidence of credibility than any other faith system. The Bible was written by about forty authors over a period of fifteen hundred years and covered a period of about four thousand years. Since the time of Jesus, more than a million people have willingly died for Him. That was mind-boggling to me. I wanted this Jesus, but I needed a complete break from this business – and I didn't have it yet.

But Nufo was right. I was still in the middle of a lot of activity. I was still involved with transporting drugs and making transactions. I still had a delivery to make.

I noted the road sign – Detroit 500 miles. In eight hours we would be delivering a load of dope to nervous people wearing guns. *We gotta get back to business.* Deep down, though, I knew that the only business worth getting back to was Jesus.

Chapter 11

Trouble with Rizzo

Lazy Su's Fish and Chips
June 1998

I had introduced Rizzo to Lazy Su about four months earlier. Su had always been reliable and found good product for me, and now she was doing the same for Rizzo. He mostly took care of his guy in Detroit, but he had found another customer in North Carolina whom he wanted to supply.

I was told that Rizzo had stopped in to talk to Lazy Su, but she was busy. He heard enough of the conversation to know that she was having supply issues.

"Problems?" Rizzo asked.

"Got shorted on a load to South Dakota and Jose's threatening to pop me if it ever happens again. I gotta eat ten grand on this one."

"My guess is Munchian jacked this up for you. Since he turned Jesus freak, he's jacking everything he touches."

Su didn't know how much to trust Rizzo, but admitted, "Yeah, it was Roger."

"You need to break from him."

"Roger says you're dangerous the way you push so hard to get new supply. One wrong move and we're done."

"And this is coming from Roger?"

"Yeah. I know you need a load, Rizzo, but I'm working on one for Roger right now. It's high stakes – five hundred pounds up to Simen."

"When's the load scheduled to go?"

"Next month."

"Tell me about it. Tell me all about it."

So Rizzo got the details of my load at the time he needed one for North Carolina.

Provo, Utah

July 1998

My big load to Detroit ran into major problems. Nufo was running it, and I trusted him. However, I never expected him to be tailed and hijacked, but I learned later that despite all his precautions, he was ambushed.

He was being watched even as Su's guys loaded the duffel bags into the Mountaineer. Five hundred pounds of fresh harvest was a lot to stuff into the tight space behind the false speakers, but they did it, and Nufo pulled out of Su's driveway and began his meandering through the streets. His tail managed to stay with him through Phoenix, and even maintained a five-car distance on the interstate. I had trained Nufo to continually check his mirrors for a tail, but at that distance, he could not recognize anything amiss.

After dark, the tail closed in on him for nine hours until Nufo pulled off the highway and into the parking lot of a Motel 6. He crawled into the passenger seat to catch some sleep without leaving the load unattended. The tail parked at the other end of the parking lot and waited. Two hours later, though, Nufo was cornered by Mo and three of his buddies. He should have walked away and given up the load, but Nufo tried out his fancy footwork and put up his dukes – only these guys weren't interested in boxing.

Nufo was fast and blocked a series of punches, and then he flattened Mo with a counterpunch. Two of the others joined in the fight until their friend got up and produced a bicycle chain from his back pocket. Nufo managed to swipe away the first couple swings until Mo wrapped the chain around his head. Then it was over. He whirled Nufo around and slammed him into the Mountaineer. Then they all got in the fight with their knees to Nufo's body and blows to his head. Nufo collapsed to the ground, and the kicks and blows continued.

Eventually, they quit. It was over. The tail started his ignition and drove forward. Mo walked up to the vehicle. "Gutsy little dude, I gotta give him that," he said.

"Is he still breathing?"

"A little. What should we do with him?"

"Stick him in the trunk and gift wrap him – special delivery to Munchian's front door," he said as he walked over to the Mountaineer and got in.

Mo and his guys gathered Nufo up and tucked him into the trunk of the car. Sitting in the Mountaineer, Rizzo watched in the mirror as Mo slammed the trunk and went to the back of the Mountaineer. He popped the hatch.

"Load's all here. You're set to go."

Mo climbed behind the wheel of Rizzo's car and took off. Rizzo didn't expect that the rip-off would cost Nufo his life, but then again, he didn't really care. Rizzo cranked the engine and took off. He had a client in North Carolina to make happy.

My doorbell rang. Car tires screeched out of my driveway as I opened the door and saw Nufo's blood-soaked body on my porch.

"I had to break you again, Roger."

Yes, I experienced being broken again when I opened that front door and saw Nufo as a pulpy mess on my porch. I relived that moment when I stepped out from the wreckage of my car and saw death surrounding me. I had nowhere to run and nowhere to hide.

"I have great plans for you, Roger. Trust Me."

Nufo was in the hospital as his brain was searching for his identity through the fluid that filled his skull. I visited him every day and relived the moment I had stood over Alma's bed, staring down at the damage I had done to one of God's creations. My friend, Nufo – he was in there somewhere, but the doctors couldn't guarantee that he would come out again. For three days, I didn't go home. I slept on the vinyl bench in the lobby. Once I got home, I saw my pager on my desk. I had missed more than fifty pages from Simen. The deadline for the delivery had come and gone.

Four days later, my leg collapsed as I walked down the hall toward Nufo's room, and I became a patient in the hospital myself. The surgeons literally had to re-break my knee. I had neglected it after it was shattered in the accident, and it healed wrong. The doctor told me that the only way to ever gain normal use of my knee again was for them to go in, re-break it, and then repair it the way it should have been done in the first place.

"Why didn't you come in right away?" the doctor asked me.

"I'm not sure why," was all I could say.

"A thing like this really needed surgical attention immediately. I can fix it, but your recovery will be longer and more painful. You will require more therapy in order to regain full use."

"When can you schedule the surgery?"

"I suggest as soon as possible. Man, you really should have let a surgeon handle this sooner."

The surgeon was eager to get at my leg – hacking and breaking. The doctor had been right. Recovery was more painful than anything I had ever experienced, and it didn't have to be this way. If I had done the right thing, recovery would have been faster without so much pain, and the scars would not have been as deep. I should have listened to the doctor. I should also have listened to the Master Surgeon, the One who wanted my attention.

So now I was bedridden. The pager buzzed continually on my nightstand. I ignored it, knowing that it was another page from Simen. Rizzo had ripped him off, and Simen was not happy that I had failed to come through as usual. I took care of the whole thing financially, but the Chaldean drug cartel had a reputation of ruthlessness that it had to keep. They took rip-offs personally, regardless of who ate the cost.

As I was recovering, God brought back to me the memory of my first drug bust – the night the cop told me he would call my parents at the airport and tell them I would be ten to fifteen years late. That was my first time in a Maricopa County tank – with a junkie named Cisco curled up in the corner. I heard him say, "You know, when God's got a lesson to teach you, He sends you a teacher." I remember looking at the balding older guy propped up against the cinder-block wall. He had a whitewashed face and a defeated smile, but there was a twinkle in his eyes.

"Excuse me?" I said.

"That's what my grandmother used to tell me whenever I'd get in trouble. 'God has a lesson for you,' and now forty-five years later, I get it."

"Nice. Thanks for sharing."

With his mouth twitching and leg trembling, the junkie rolled over. Somewhere in the back of my mind, I wondered if I was looking at my future.

"You've gone this route before," he said.

I told him I wasn't in the mood for talking.

"Strange. Neither am I. But something told me that I needed to talk to you. What Grandma meant was that the teacher was my consequences."

"No kidding. Took you forty-five years to figure it out?"

"God let them happen to teach me a lesson."

I remember saying, "God's a spectator in my life. If that's the way He operates, He can just stay on the sidelines." I wanted to dim that guy's lights, but he was too old and pathetic to pop.

"Took me forty-five years. Frank over there," he said as he pointed to another junkie, "he ain't figured it out yet. It's too late for him. He probably won't make it through the night. Took me forty-five. How long's it gonna take you?"

"Okay, super genius, how's God teaching you now? You're back in the zoo."

The old man went on about how God had given him a time-out to make him think about the direction of his life. He said he saw two guys stick another guy's head in a drain and snap his neck. He said he didn't want that, but he was back in the tank, looking at ten years. That thought sobered him up a little, and he got quiet the rest of the night.

By morning, Cisco the junkie was dead.

The sound of my pager brought me back to the present. It was Simen. I ignored it. Then it went off again, and I decided to look at it. It was Chico. That meant business. I reached for the phone. *When God's got a lesson to teach you, He sends a teacher.*

I touched the receiver. *God gives warnings. I wish I would have listened.*

I picked up the receiver, ready to dial. I knew that with one more dial, one more delivery, I could get out of my problem. Just one more deal.

"When are you going to listen to Me?"

I hung up the phone and stared at the pager. It lit up again. Simen. It lit up yet again. Chico. Wow! Chico never called twice.

"Trust Me, Roger. Trust Me."

I grabbed the water glass on the nightstand and crushed the pager with it. The glass broke in my hand. I stared at the blood dripping from my palm. Blood had dripped from the hands of Christ, too, only He had shed His blood by His decision to obey God.

Okay, God, You got me.

Only later would I learn that during this time, Rizzo proved to be as dangerous as I had feared. He met a new connection at Martini Ranch – a guy he had been told could provide large. The guy introduced himself as Papian, and he ordered bourbon straight up. They retreated to the courtyard where it was quieter for business.

As they stood next to the high-top tables, Papian listened intently to Rizzo rattle off about me. True to form, Rizzo went on and on, flapping his lips about how great things had been and were getting bigger in Detroit and North Carolina. In his efforts to sound like a big shot, he spilled his guts about his business and said that I was washed out, having lost my last shipment. Drinking his fifth vodka, Rizzo worked hard to impress Papian.

Then Papian dug deeper with questions about me. "I know all the players. Don't give me no straw man to make yourself look bigger. I don't deal with anyone who isn't in my league. If I find out you ain't in my league, we got problems. If you get a real clear understanding of that up front, sport, you're gonna be okay."

"Hey, I ain't jacking you around about Munchian. The guy's slick, real cool about his business. At least he used to be."

They ended the conversation after Rizzo told him what he needed up in Detroit. Papian said he needed twenty-four hours. They exchanged cell-phone numbers and pagers, with Rizzo giving him all the numbers he reserved for business purposes only. Then Papian left. As Rizzo reached for his next drink, he noticed that Papian's glass of bourbon was still full. He had never touched it.

Special Agent Papian from the Detroit field office of the Drug Enforcement Agency slid behind the wheel of his Suburban. He booted up his computer and called in to give the order for electronic surveillance on the cell-phone number and pager that Rizzo had given him. Because Rizzo had told him that these were used exclusively for business, he also had probable cause to tap every outgoing and incoming number. Within hours, his analysts would have a complete list of calls and pages from the last month.

Rizzo's idiocy had made him the prime target in an investigation, but his big mouth implicated a lot of other people. Papian's surveillance team quickly came up with a list of suspected offenders (legal names have been changed) and their suspected offenses:

Rizzo

- Conspiracy
- Illegally conducting an enterprise
- Possession of marijuana for sale

Robby the Jew

- Illegally conducting an enterprise
- Possession of marijuana for sale

Simon B.

- Possession of marijuana for sale

Big Mama Su

- Possession of marijuana for sale

Gibby

- Transport for sale, sale or transport of marijuana

Mo

- Transport for sale, sale or transport of marijuana

Papian stared at the list of players and visualized the list growing rapidly as the investigation unfolded. Thanks to Rizzo, the wiretaps alone had the potential of snagging at least a dozen more. At the moment, the meeting gave him one new name, and Papian sensed it was significant:

Hrach R. Munchian (a.k.a. Roger Rabbit)

- Conspiracy
- Illegally conducting an enterprise
- Possession of marijuana for sale

He shut down his laptop and smiled. He was about to catch a cartoon bunny. He was closing in to snag Roger Rabbit – me.

Part 3

God Redeems

Chapter 12

Rizzo's Fall; My About-Face

Phoenix
September 1998

The medications eased the pain of my shattered knee, but they could not silence the haunting nightmares of death: *Strapped to the chair, heavy door slams, stench of vomit, bile, and urine lace the dark cell. An endless struggle against restraints. Unearthly cries of anguish echo off cinder-block walls. So tired. I can't fight anymore.*

Oh, God, help! My cry bounced off the plaster walls as I sat straight up in bed. My sheets were drenched and my body glistened in sweat. I checked the time. It was 2:22 p.m. My Bible lay face down on my chest, stuck in a pool of sweat. I peeled it off. Deuteronomy 8 was soaked. My pain medication must have knocked me out as I was reading. God's Word was now imprinted dead center on my chest. Amazed, I remembered what Deuteronomy 6:8 had said: *Tie them as symbols on your hands and bind them on your foreheads.*

Well, God, I said to myself, *it's not exactly my forehead, but Your Word is bound to me now.*

I reached for my crutches and wobbled out of bed. It was two months after the surgery, and the pain was as fresh as the day they re-broke my knee and put it back together. The surgeon had to

remove a ligament from my right calf to replace the shredded ligament in my left knee. I made it to the kitchen and found some cold
pizza and stale Coke. The phone rang as I waited for the microwave
to zap my pizza. I checked the caller ID. It was another collection
call. I ignored it.

I sat down with my flat Coke and sizzling pizza and downed two
painkillers. The phone rang again, and again I ignored it, knowing
that they would only try twice. I grabbed the letter on the table from
Parker & Sons Law Firm, recommended by Jay, who had successfully saved me from twenty years of prison as a result of the accident.
Instead, we won a plea deal of five years' intense probation.

Pastor Frank had reminded me that God had been protecting me.
"God has been with you all along. He wants to work through you.
Just think back to see where God has spared and protected you." I
knew he was right. The letter from the law firm confirmed that my
bankruptcy petition had been filed. Jay didn't do bankruptcies. The
collection calls should stop soon. Then the phone rang again. They
never call three times, so I looked. My stomach sank. It was from
Detroit: Simen.

God had broken me, but I had tried to seek God while clinging to
my worldly things. Just like my shattered knee, I didn't heal so well. I
wanted to keep everything from my life of drugs, sex, and violence.
God had to re-break me, and He used Rizzo to do it with that load
that was meant for Simen. If I had not had that Damascus moment
in the rat-infested jail cell, I would have popped Rizzo within twenty-
four hours and then would have popped Mo and his friends too. But
God breaks us for a reason. He calls us for His work.

I knew I could not keep up with the lifestyle of the criminal world.
God was blessing the family insurance business. It was growing in
ways I could not explain. However, I also knew that I could easily
pick up the phone and score more in one call than I could in a whole
year of signing new insurance clients. Even worse, my connections
were betting that this religious awakening was only a temporary

Bible-thumping phase. My phone rang constantly. Temptation was always there. As I looked at the bankruptcy papers, I knew that one call could put me back at the Empire Night Club and back into positive cash flow – back in the game.

I had been ignoring Simen's calls for several weeks. After I smashed my pager, Simen couldn't send me any coded messages. I don't remember how, but I found myself dressed and in my car, heading for the pay phone from which I could return Simen's call.

"So, are you really doing this?" Simen's voice came through the line. "I get a little nervous when guys like you, at the top of their game, think they're gonna get out. Feds love guys like you, and I gotta think that the best thing for me is if I see them hanging from a bridge somewhere."

"I'm doing this, Simen. I'm out."

"I got a guy up in Washington State. Spokane. He's looking for a good connection. Three or four loads a month, about two hundred and fifty pounds a pop. I could give him to you. You get your guy Nufo back on the road, and you're in business."

"Just to clarify, we *are* square, right, Simen? I ate it on that last load. Sorry it didn't work out, but it was my investment I lost. We're square, right? I really don't wanna spend the rest of my life looking over my shoulder waiting for one of your homies to give me a .22-caliber headache."

"Yeah, I hear you. How's your boy Nufo?"

"Recovering. He'll pull through."

"I hear the guys who done that are still above ground. As a going-away present, I could take care of that for you."

"If I wanted it done, I would have done it myself."

"I have a guy with a palm gun. Rizzo would never see it coming."

"Rizzo wouldn't see a freight train coming. Thanks anyway."

"Even as a crook, your word has been your bond – like being an honest crook. I guess that's why you're still alive and why you aren't dangling from some bridge. I can trust you. I just hope you don't give me an uneasy feeling in the future, especially, you know, if your past catches up with you. Because it will. The past always catches up to you."

"My focus is on my relationship with God now."

"Well, let's hope we don't have to find out how big your God is. Good luck to you, my friend."

I no longer worried about such veiled threats. I trusted a big God now – a God whose word would never return empty to Him. Nothing was impossible for Him.

Simen still thought of me as a drug dealer – an honest one – but as Romans 8:16-17 came to mind, I knew that the Holy Spirit was teaching me differently: *The Spirit himself testifies with our spirit that we are God's children. Now if we are children, then we are heirs – heirs of God and co-heirs with Christ, if indeed we share in his sufferings in order that we may also share in his glory.*

I was no longer a drug dealer. I was not a criminal. I was not a murderer. Jesus Christ shed His blood for me, so I became an heir to God's kingdom. The Spirit also confirmed that if we are to share Christ's kingdom, we are also to share in His sufferings. I knew that God was preparing me for battle, but I did not understand this new war. However, I experienced a peace like I had never felt before. I had a lot to learn, but I was ready to take up my cross and accept whatever circumstances God wanted to use to train me.

I found it fitting that my Damascus moment had come at dawn, and the day ahead brightened. What I didn't know was that dark days were closing in on me during which the battle would be fought.

Detroit

Unknown to me at the time, while I was cutting ties with Simen, Special Agent Papian doggedly pursued me. When he received a call from Detroit Police Detective Fredericks about information on the Simen wiretap, he jumped at the chance to meet with him.

Per Fredericks's food preferences, they met at Lafayette Coney Island where he could indulge in Coney dogs with everything. Papian passed on the dogs, but wanted the information. He knew Fredericks had good reason for hating drugs and drug dealers. Some bad seed had erased the mind of Fredericks's sixteen-year-old son when the boy had experimented with the dope at a party. Papian knew this gave Fredericks the kind of style and gut-level vitriol that was needed in his narcotics division.

While Fredericks was motivated to bring Simen down, Papian wanted to nail me. He knew I was well connected and hoped I would lead him to bigger fish, but I had dropped off the radar shortly after the team had infiltrated the ring of cartels through Rizzo. My connection to Rizzo was still unclear to him, but it was the only solid link he had to Simen.

Papian sat on a stool next to Fredericks. "So what have you got for me?"

"Munchian finally took a call from Simen."

"You get it on tape?"

Fredericks shook his head and picked up his second dog. "Simen's been dialing Munchian's digits nonstop. Munchian didn't take any of his calls until yesterday morning. They got a system worked out. Our team observed Munchian leaving his house yesterday, and they tailed him to a pay phone matching previous calls to Simen. Based on phone records, his move correlated with the last time he and Simen connected. Both pay phones were sterile, so we got nothing on record, but we know they talked."

"Okay. They talked. We got something."

Fredericks shook his head. "My suggestion is to drop the Munchian thing. It's a bad angle for you to work. These two guys – neither will give the other up. Munchian got all whacked out on religion and decided that salvation would come by splitting from the cartel. Who's he kidding? That's a death sentence – especially dealing with guys like Simen. The Chaldean cartel has a reputation of making things very painful if you cross them. Munchian knows that, but somehow Simen respects him, and now they're done."

"What makes you think neither of these guys can be rattled?"

"You need to focus on Rizzo. He'll flap his jaws for a dime, but I'd suggest you move in fast. His days are numbered. He got involved with China Mike, Jamaican-born with squinty eyes."

"We've got more intel to gather on Rizzo before we move. Keep digging on the Simen angle."

"Bring Rizzo in. Show him he's looking at doing a dime apiece up the street, and he'll turn on his Aunt Tillie to save his hide."

Papian tossed some cash on the counter and stood to leave. Fredericks said, "Rizzo's shelf life has about four to five months left. China Mike's angling to do a number on him soon. We gotta get what we can. No one hates them more than I do."

"I know."

"Drugs poison minds. They erase lives – young lives. Drug dealers, guys like Munchian, they should all go down for murder. They feed young kids the stuff that takes away their dreams and their futures."

"You sure about Munchian going religious?"

"Yeah."

Papian had an extra-difficult time dealing with those who went religious after making millions. He didn't believe in a God who would let someone like me walk.

Fredericks said, "I know you don't like me. I know you don't like the way I do things, but I want you to understand the way it is and where I'm coming from. You got to the Munchian party too late. God got there first."

"Stay on Munchian and Simen. I'm not ready to hang that one up yet."

Grand Lake, Colorado
October 1998

While Fredericks and Papian planned for my demise, I learned that the moron Rizzo had set himself up for a big fall. He bought a house in Grand Lake, Colorado, and accumulated a ski boat from a connection who couldn't pay. With two new drivers, Jimmy and Gibby, running loads from Phoenix to China Mike's guys in Detroit, the house was centrally located. As Rizzo sat in the spotter's seat, he realized what a bunch of dangerous idiots he was mixed up with.

After ripping off my load, I know Rizzo was always looking over his shoulder. He expected me to come up behind him with one of my pistols and put him in permanent retirement. He knew I had turned to God, and he didn't quite know what to make of it. He figured I'd get popped soon anyway, which is common for those who leave the business. Getting out by getting religion made too many people nervous.

I could have told Rizzo that he was playing with fire, but Rizzo thought he was pretty hot stuff. Now he was working with Mo, who was nuts. Mo introduced him to China Mike, whose customers were high maintenance and demanding. His two drivers were not the brightest either. His worry about me taking him out faded as he dealt with Mo and China Mike.

Phoenix

The time is quite blurry in my memory, but I remember deciding to visit pastor Frank's church, which is in the Sunnyslope community of Phoenix – not a good neighborhood. This was a brand-new thing for me – a Pentecostal denomination church. For some reason, God started me with the Pentecostal experience. I didn't know any church politics or understand the different denominations and belief systems. This was my first experience after all those years of my Orthodox, or Catholic-like, experience.

I had a lot of issues with what I saw at Pastor Frank's church. I was not comfortable with the speaking in tongues, the altar calls, the sinner's prayer, pushing down, and all kinds of stuff. I didn't know anything about this, so I was walking in blindly. I thought, *Okay, what is this?* It was news to me, but it was all I had at the time. I couldn't accept it because it felt weird. I liked the messages, though. They were clear and simple, and I liked that.

I attended regularly, learned praise songs, and absorbed the Word of God as Pastor Frank preached. My knee was not 100 percent healed yet, but I was no longer bedridden. I hobbled with a cane as I learned to walk again. Just like learning to walk physically, my new spiritual walk with God was a daily struggle. I did not want to live my old life anymore. I also knew that I wanted to learn more about my heavenly Father, who seemed to love me enough to come to my rescue in a rat-hole jail cell when I was strapped to a black crazy chair on wheels. That night, I was rescued – not arrested.

The morning service was over, and the church was empty. I sat there alone, close to the front, but not quite in the front row. I thought about Pastor Frank's message from Psalm 139. He spoke about God's thoughts and about how deeply God thinks of us. He said that God searched me and knew my thoughts. God's thoughts outnumbered the grains of sand on the earth. I realized that His knowledge was too wonderful for me. God has loved me because God is love. That is indescribable.

As I sat there, I felt an urge to go to the altar. I slipped out of the pew and knelt with my elbows on the railing. I tried to pray, but I had no words. Finally I prayed, *God, what is it that You want? God, where do I start?*

Suddenly I felt a gentle hand on my shoulder, and someone knelt next to me. I looked and saw John and his wife, Glenda, who were church members.

"What keeps you inside today, Roger?"

"I was just thinking about the message. I'm lost. I want so badly to follow God. I'm not doing something right, and I can't figure out what it is."

"A newborn doesn't learn to walk overnight," Glenda said.

I looked at the cross, and tears flooded my cheeks. "I don't know where to start. I come to church and I read God's Word every day, but sometimes I just don't get what I'm reading. There's so much to understand."

"You don't have to understand everything you read in God's Word, Roger. Just thirst for His Word and let its power feed your spirit. Don't get discouraged."

Glenda asked, "Roger, have you accepted Christ as your Savior?"

"I guess so. I think so. I thought I did – that night I was strapped in the nut chair in the county jail. That was a moment of truth for me. That was my awakening. It was real with no other men involved – like Saul with his encounter with God on the Damascus Road."

John said, "Consider Pastor Frank's message today about God's thoughts – a God who thinks of every person, every individual, regardless of what they have done, of how lost they are, and of how far away they seem. A God whose daily thoughts outnumber the grains of sand on the earth is a God who would do anything to have a relationship with you – and He did. He sent His only Son to die on a cross so that through His blood, your sins would be washed clean, and through His resurrection, He could build a relationship with you. *God made him who had no sin to be sin for us, so that in him we might become the righteousness of God* (2 Corinthians 5:21)."

That's when I realized that I had to begin a real and personal relationship with the only One who did not reject me, but I had to really know Him and had to believe that what I believed was really true so that I could commit my life to Him. John and Glenda prayed for me. I think they felt compelled to lead me to Christ. I didn't really know what I was doing. I was emotional and may have just gone along with the flow. I realized later that it wasn't real, but was just an emotional moment. I had good intentions, but it had nothing to do with my commitment to Christ.

I recalled Simen's words when he told me that even as a crook, I was an honest crook. Even as a crook, my word was my bond. It was an unbreakable commitment. Now I had made a commitment with the Lord Jesus Christ, who had shed His blood and suffered to pay the price for all the awful and atrocious things I had done. I realized that Simen had spared my life because of my word, and I now realized that I could have eternal life because of God's Word. I felt the chains of a decade of crime, arrest, and incarceration fall from me. I was filled with joy, and I felt the peace that surpasses all understanding (Philippians 4:7).

Detroit, Michigan
December 1998
While I was getting right with God, Rizzo was messing up big time. He played the tough guy as he tried to break ties with Mo and China Mike. Then he shafted Gibby and refused to pay him his ten thousand for making a run. He blamed it on Mo by saying that Mo's customers refused to pay. Rizzo owed him one more load and that was to be it.

When Gibby went to settle things with Mo, he heard how it really went down. Mo asked him, "So, you wanna get double your money plus a bonus?"

"I'm listening."

Mo had a plan to get Gibby paid double and rattle Rizzo. They would ask for Paulette to deliver the money and pull a fast one on her, leaving her high and dry. They included Rizzo in the plan to distract Paulette, and Rizzo ended up losing two Suburbans and the money.

January 1999
I wanted to change my life, but connections from my past continued to work the business – the business that I had been intimately involved in – and that meant there could still be consequences. While Rizzo persisted in making a mess of things, Papian and Fredericks concentrated on the big bust.

The courier delivered two envelopes to Special Agent Papian as he sat watching the blizzard from his office. He envied the U.S. marshals in Phoenix who, by the stroke of the judge's pen, had just received authority to make their move. His gut told him he was pulling the pin on this operation too soon, but he had no choice. Detective Fredericks was right. Rizzo was in trouble with China Mike and friends, and now he was in deep with the heavies out of Mexico. They could pop him anytime. Things were falling apart fast, so it was time to bring him in. There was no way to protect him from the Mexican armor about to be trained on him.

The envelopes contained copies of the arrest warrants issued out of the United States District Court, Eastern District of Michigan. There was one for Rizzo and one for Paulette. Then the phone rang.

"Papian."

Special Agent Jane Hensley's voice came through the line: "Morning, David. Federal marshals are making their move on the Phoenix residence of Rizzo."

Hensley was a special agent who worked for the ruthless female attorney general, Billie Rosen. Billie was every drug dealer's nightmare. She was famous for arranging steep bail on traffickers and keeping them locked up in the county hole while stringing their case along in legal red tape. She was also famous for turning more punks into informants than any other prosecutor in Arizona. Getting snared by Billie Rosen became known as getting caught in the "JAP trap" – Jewish American Princess.

After it was obvious that the wiretaps were going nowhere, Fredericks suggested that Papian drop the whole thing and let it go to State. "Let me know when they're both in custody," he said.

Chapter 13

Arrest, Release, and Uncertainty

Federal Prison Camp
February 1999

I got word that Rizzo had been wearing tan shirts and pants for the last month, cleaning crusted, filthy latrines at Nellis Air Force Base. The prison provided labor to support the base, and Rizzo was there looking at too many years working without pay while scrubbing stainless steel toilet bowls.

Federal marshals had shown up at Rizzo's front door with their Glocks holstered and wearing their blue windbreakers with a yellow star stenciled on the front and "Police" stenciled below. It all went down on January 14. Four official sedans were parked in his driveway as the marshals knocked politely on his door and told him they had a warrant for his arrest as well as one for Paulette. Rizzo and Paulette were soon cuffed and on their way to the Federal Building downtown.

Rizzo got dumped into a Maricopa County hold until they transported him up to Nevada, where he met Special Agent Papian. What a shock it was for Rizzo! He recognized Papian immediately. He tried to cover his face in disbelief, but the chains that tethered him to the table prevented his arms from moving to his face.

Papian showed him the charges and told him he was looking at

121 months unless he cooperated. "Your testimony about Munchian ain't lining up with your squeeze Paulette's story."

"Well, Paulette really wasn't involved."

"Okay, Rizzo. Here's how it is. I'm going to bust Roger. I'm going to bust a lot of people based on what you tell me here. So if I decide I can't trust you, you'll be spending the next ten years cleaning toilets. I have more than eighteen potential co-conspirators who can get me the information I need, so you need to decide now. Are you going to provide me with it or do I need to plan my travel to other places?".

"Okay." Rizzo said. "What do you really want to know about Roger Munchian?"

"Tell me everything. The truth this time."

August 1999

Within the first year of attending Pastor Frank's church, I discovered he had his own problems, which in turn shook my new faith. The church closed down, and lots of people turned their backs on him.

This was all very disappointing. I wasn't even sure if I was a baby Christian yet. I was devastated when the church closed and everyone bashed Frank. The ugliness of the treatment that Frank received shook me. I was witnessing not only truth in this church, but I also saw the ugliness of this church. The people talked about forgiveness, but couldn't even forgive their own pastor. It was mind-boggling to me. I didn't know what to make of it, but I know one thing: I was the only person to come alongside him to comfort and support him during this time of his life. He was alone and depressed. I tried to cheer him up, and I invited him on a trip to Los Angeles with me in hope of getting his mind off his problem.

My limousine driver (yes, I lived a pretty enabled life) drove me to nightclubs and elsewhere. He knew my status and who I was. He told me that his dad pastored a Pentecostal church called Amor Outreach. I was still weaning off the business, disconnecting with cartels, doing less of my crime work, and searching for more of Jesus.

It was an equalizing moment. I did less and less business and more and more Jesus. I have come to believe that when most become a Christian, they are not immediately sinless; they just sin less as they learn more and grow in Christ.

The limousine guy recommended his dad's church, even though he did not attend there. It was another small church, with about eighty people attending. Pastor Zeke was a great speaker with great emotion, but I had issues with the same Pentecostal methods. I couldn't absorb what was going on around me with the tongues and people running around. It didn't make sense to me, but I didn't leave. I tried to put forth effort there because I loved the messages. They were really powerful messages. They were clear, and I could understand them.

I was so hungry for God and His truth that I started attending another church, a small Spanish church that was also Pentecostal. Pastor Pablo Contreras preached clear messages that I liked, and I also continued to learn by reading the Bible on my own. Some days it seemed as if the more I learned, the hungrier I got.

St. Louis

Both Rizzo and Paulette flapped their gums to the Feds, and the arrests were coming down. In March, the Feds showed up at Mo's house with a search warrant, and they got him not only for drugs and paraphernalia, but also for his stash of assault weapons. They found me at my office. The U.S. marshals walked right in and escorted me out in front of my employees.

They were also hot on the trail of Lazy Su. Su's brother, AB, had called her and told her it was just a matter of time before they knocked on her door. He told her to get out immediately. Plans were in the works back home for them, and all they had to do was get their travel set. But while AB was trying to get his passport squared away, the Feds showed up and hauled him in. Lazy Su wasn't going to wait. She made arrangements to get a fake passport. She booked her flight, got out of her apartment, and went to the Marriott in St. Louis under an assumed name until her fake passport was delivered.

Her accommodations at the Marriott were not bad. It was clean, continental breakfast was provided, and there was a pool.

Su was anxious, but in just a few hours she hoped to be boarding a plane and getting out of there. Her flight was in the morning. First stop, New York. Then nonstop to Paris and on to Saudi Arabia. She planned to be home in thirty-six hours. She hadn't moved any dope for several months, and she had no debts. She had sold Lazy Su's before going to St. Louis for surgery, so she had plenty of cash. She was sitting in her room smoking a cigarette and watching TV when she heard a knock at the door. She turned the light and the TV off.

There was another knock on the door. "Open the door please, Ms. Su."

Su hadn't given the hotel her real name, so she peeked through the hole and saw the manager. She said, "I have an early flight. I need to get some sleep."

"Ms. Su, please don't make me call security."

She unchained the door and opened it. Two men in blue waved gold stars with "U.S. Marshal" imprinted in the middle.

"Ms. Haddad, we have a warrant for your arrest, issued by the United States District Court, Eastern District of Michigan. We need you to come with us, please."

Phoenix

September 1999

Six months after my arrest, I pulled up to the curb at Phoenix Sky Harbor Airport. I got out and helped my parents get their luggage out of the trunk. They were headed to Armenia for two months to visit family and play matchmaker for me. Now that this case – something they really did not understand – was done and dismissed, they wanted me to meet someone and settle down. My last marriage had failed, and they figured it was because I had married an Americanized Armenian. They thought I needed a sweet Armenian girl who had not been influenced by the selfish, materialistic culture of America.

My parents had wanted to take this trip several months ago, but I had stalled them because I was uncertain of the outcome of my legal problems. They were aware that I was in some sort of trouble because I was always talking on the phone to that lawyer back in Michigan and was constantly traveling back and forth to Detroit. I always told them I had a "meeting" back there.

It was hard to believe that it had been six months since it all went down. That sunny Monday morning (March 15), I had been in my office at Diamondback Insurance with my Bible resting on the corner of my desk and a crown of thorns hanging from a nail on the wall to remind me of the price that was paid for me. I heard a commotion out front and heard my assistant saying, "Yes, he's back in his office."

Then there was a knock on the door. I answered, "Come in."

My tiny office was suddenly filled with DEA officers, federal marshals, Arizona DPS officers, and U.S. Customs officers. They escorted me out, tucked me into a government sedan, and took me to the Federal Building. They informed me of the charges that came from the U.S. Federal Eastern District Court Detroit. My arrest record stated that the prosecutors in this case had federal witnesses, Rizzo and Paulette, in custody, who were willing to testify to my involvement in conspiracy and drug trafficking. I was allowed to review the charges, and I knew this was serious. There were twelve class 2 felony charges. Two of the counts were for conspiracy and for conducting an illegal enterprise, and the rest were for possession of marijuana for sale or transfer. Class 2 meant twenty to life. I quickly added it up to 160 years.

I felt as if I was back in the Madison Street hold again, looking at spending the rest of my life in prison.

"Trust Me, Roger. Trust Me."

I was surprised when I was told that I was being released on my own recognizance, but I was required to surrender my passport. I would be notified of my first hearing date in Detroit. By lunchtime, I was back in my office calling Jay.

Jay recommended Frank Marcello, an Italian attorney up in Detroit who specialized in federal cases. I flew to Detroit to meet him at his office. He put it to me straight. He said, "Yeah, this is serious. The gig was a joint task force of the DEA, U.S. Customs, and the Narcotics Division of the Detroit Police Department. The Drug Enforcement Division of the Arizona AG also had their noses cocked in this direction, so watch your back once I get you cut loose from this."

These were not encouraging words, but then he went on to say, "How much confidence you got that this Rizzo guy's got the goods on you?"

"Rizzo?" I tried not to laugh.

"I get it. He's a low-level. That's what I figured. He's got nothing on you but what his little pea-brain can concoct. Okay. Here's the way it is. They had been on Rizzo for nearly a year up until '98 when the moron arranged a buy from the DEA's lead investigator, Agent Papian. This is what's going to happen. You're going to meet with Papian. He's going to play hardball and try to get you to deal to turn government witness. He'll paint an ugly picture of you spending the rest of your life in a federal hole. You don't have to say a word, and I advise you not to say a word. The Feds don't have a tight lid on you. Keep tight-lipped, show up for all of your hearings, and let me do my thing in the courts. We'll get you untangled from this, capiche? Hey, when we walk out of that court for the last time, I'll take you down to Little Italy and we'll celebrate at Roma Café."

When I finally met Papian, God's true grace was revealed. He painted an ugly picture and told me about the eighteen conspirators in custody. He started naming them. I knew some of them real well, but others I had only heard of. As I listened, I realized that everything the Feds had on the cartel happened after I got out – after I had made my decision to turn to God. The accident in 1997 was more than God's way of getting my attention. God stopped me in that crumpled heap and used the wreckage to keep me from a lifetime of incarceration.

I stayed true to Marcello's counsel, flying to Detroit every month and never missing a court date. At the end of August, the Feds dropped the case against me, and Marcello took me down to Roma's in Little Italy; we celebrated. Marcello drank a $200 bottle of Gaja Barbaresco by himself while I stuck to my glass of water and lemon.

All of that had cleared the way for my parents to make their trip to Armenia. I pulled away from the curb at Sky Harbor and watched them in the rearview mirror as they faded away. As I drove along I-10, my pager went off. I had gotten a new one for legitimate business only, so I was shocked to see that it was from Simen. I had no idea how he got my number. I pulled off.

"Okay, first off, you gotta know that Rizzo's a dead man. I don't care where he ends up. I got people all over."

"That's your way, not mine, Simen. Is that what you called me about?"

"No. I wanted to thank you for holding true. You could have caused a lot of trouble for me. We could have caused a lot of trouble for each other."

"Did they dismiss your case too?"

"They dismissed everybody's. Rizzo wasn't worth much. Last I heard, the Feds reneged on his deal. He's looking at a ten-year stretch, no time served."

"Too bad. I appreciate you, Simen, but I think this is it for us, okay? I don't see any reason for our paths to cross again."

"I wouldn't be so sure about that."

"What do you mean?"

"Just watch yourself, okay? The Feds may have dismissed this, but that doesn't mean the state of Arizona can't pick it up."

"State charges?"

"The ride ain't done yet, buddy. Good luck."

I walked back to my car and wondered if it was too soon for my parents to be traveling to Armenia to find me a bride.

Chapter 14

Communication with Sirarpi

Yerevan, Armenia
April 2000

After my parents returned to the United States, they told me about Sirarpi, and I decided to place the call to Armenia and talk to her. The day I called, her neighbor knocked on her door and told her that she had a phone call – a long-distance call from the United States. Her family didn't have a phone at the time, so their neighbors were kind enough to let them use their phone for emergencies.

I introduced myself as Hrach, but my fluency with the Armenian language was strained. I had grown up in America and had not been back to Armenia. Sirarpi had heard about the United States through her uncle who lived in California, but she had never been here.

As we talked, she put the pieces together. Earlier that month, my parents had gone with her parents to her workplace to introduce themselves. They told her that they were distant cousins of her uncle and that they had dropped by her house to visit her parents and wanted to meet her. My parents were jovial and talked about how long it had been since they had visited their country.

Their story was common enough. They'd had an opportunity to get out of Armenia more than twenty years ago through the luck of the draw in a lottery that granted their household visas. Opportunities to return were rare and were only for the affluent, even after the collapse of the Soviet empire. Although the iron grip of communism eased after Armenia gained its independence from the Soviet Union, the country remained war-torn as tension with Azerbaijan escalated into a bloody six-year war that paralyzed the Armenian infrastructure with rationed gas, constant blackouts, and food shortages. Armenia was not at the top of the list for family vacation destinations.

As times got better after the war, my parents told her that their son, Hrach, wanted them to have a chance to go back and visit friends and family, so he arranged for their travel. Of course, they spoke highly of me and told her how proud they were of me rising from the dirt-poor streets of Armenia to the ghettos of Los Angeles to becoming a successful businessman in Phoenix. They took lots of pictures, making sure she was in every group shot. At the time, she did not understand why they wanted so many pictures of her in the shop, but as we spoke, she figured it out. They had come to play matchmaker.

She said that my faith and talk about God was what drew her to me. Armenians considered themselves Orthodox Christians simply by their nationality. The country, nestled between a region of godless communism and theocratic radical Islamic republics, had proclaimed itself a Christian country twelve years before the Roman Empire converted to Christianity.

Armenian history indicates that the apostles Bartholomew and Thaddeus ventured north to Armenia after the ascension of Christ. They went with nothing but the gospel, and they changed Armenian history. Because of them, Armenia was the first nation to declare itself a Christian nation, even though most Armenians did not know God personally. They knew God as a name, and they worshipped on holidays and special occasions by lighting candles. However, when Sirarpi was sixteen, she came to know a different God – a God who loved her, a God who answered prayers, a God who heals hurts and wipes away tears.

This happened shortly after her mama had become seriously ill. Because of her mama's prolonged and worsening weakness, Sirarpi feared for her mama's life and didn't want to lose her. She prayed and found a God who comforted her and gave her peace in the midst of uncertainty. God spared her mama from death, and she grew stronger as the days progressed.

Sirarpi had to seek her relationship with God in secret, though, because having such a relationship was mocked by her family and relatives. She had no choice but to go to underground worship services whenever she could sneak away. She determined that if she was ever going to marry, she was going to seek a man of God – a man who loved Jesus Christ the way she did.

After that first phone call to her, I called every day – so often that her parents finally got their own phone. She loved the fact that she could finally talk with someone about her faith. She said she was envious of me that I could openly worship at a church that loved Jesus Christ. She had to hide her Bible, but she sometimes went to "gatherings" in her town where believers worshipped Jesus in secret.

We became close friends and talked for hours at odd times due to the twelve-hour time difference. I tried to arrange for her to come to Arizona, but getting a legitimate visa out of war-torn Armenia was impossible. We even tried bribing certain people, but that didn't work either. I began looking for opportunities to go to Armenia to meet her in person. I saw that as our only option to see if we wanted to get married, but as I was moving in that direction, I was arrested again for the same RICO charges that were dismissed out of federal court in Detroit. The charges this time had been brought by the Arizona Supreme Court.

Suddenly I was not able to call Sirarpi. I couldn't even call to tell her why. My heart ached for fear of losing her and of misunderstandings that could arise. It wasn't until I stopped calling that she realized how much she cared for me. I had my mama call her and tell her I was away doing business in rural places with no access to phones. She made excuses for me to try to prevent Sirarpi from thinking I had lost interest.

One day Sirarpi decided to eat her lunch in the park, away from crowds and noise, to spend time with God. She had her Bible, but her thoughts continually turned to me. She looked up at Mt. Ararat, which reminded her of me and the way I talked about God, and it also reminded her of God's promises. She knew I was proud of my Armenian heritage. I was even proud of the prominence of that mountain in the Bible where Noah's ark came to rest when the flood waters receded.

It had been twenty-one days since I had called her. She looked down at her Bible, and the pages had blown open to Proverbs 3:5. She read, *Trust in the* Lord *with all your heart and lean not on your own understanding.*

"Okay, God," she said quietly. "I trust You, and I pray that Hrach is okay."

Madison Street Jail

It had all gone down two weeks earlier, on March 20. I had promised Sirarpi that I would call her the next morning. She would be getting home from work as my day started. I had come to love to hear her laugh. Her voice was like a kiss from God straight to my heart. We were supposed to just be friends with no expectations, but I was getting attached to her.

However, the Maricopa County Sheriff's SWAT team had crashed into my office around noon. They were not as polite as the federal marshals had been. The SWAT team, FBI, DEA, and U.S. marshals all broke in – using both the front and back doors. With their assault weapons trained on me, they slammed me to the floor, hog-tied me, and slapped handcuffs on me. My secretary was traumatized and scared to death as they dragged me from the floor and hustled me past my stunned employees and into the cruiser. My next stop was the same horseshoe at Madison St. Jail where I had been before, except my bond was half a million dollars, which I did not have. Because I had been tapering off the drug business, I no longer had that kind of cash on hand. I had disconnected from that world and had already lost a lot of money.

As I sat in the tank waiting to be processed upstairs, I recognized the cell across the hall. That was where I had been strapped to the crazy chair, where God had heard my cry in late 1997. The last time I'd faced that chair, it was dawn, and God was then answering me in my Damascus moment. The light of a new day, a new life, was ahead of me then. Now, though, I felt the darkness coming – a stormy blackness of the consequences I would face for what I had done in the past.

"Trust Me, Roger. I am here. I am with you in the calm and in the storm. I am always with you."

By midnight I was in stripes and was stretched out on the top bunk in my maximum-security cell on the third floor. My cellmate, Armando, asked, "So what kind of bail did Judge Wapner set on you?"

"Half a mil," I answered. To be exact, bail had been set at $440,000, three bills beyond my financial reach to make bond, so I was going to be there for a long time. Worse yet, there was no international calling perk at Sheriff Joe's Happy Hotel, so I couldn't even call Sirarpi to tell her what had happened. I figured it was over. Once she learned of my past, she would never have anything to do with me again. I was a criminal, a drug trafficker, a murderer.

"I am your righteousness, Roger. You are Mine, bought with the price of the blood of My only begotten Son. Don't listen to the liar. Listen to Me. Call to Me and I will answer you and tell you great and unsearchable things that you do not know."

"Half a mil? Man, they got Sammy the Bull upstairs on the fifth floor with 1.2 mil. You're in his territory!" Then Armando offered me some hooch – fermented oranges in a bag hidden in the toilet. I declined the offer, especially as I saw toilet water dripping from the bag.

So here I was for the last two weeks, and I was curious about the way Armando stood by the cell door mumbling something about getting

Sammy the Bull, who was in protective custody. "Sammy" was Salvador Gravano, the Mafia hit man who turned snitch and brought down John Gotti. He had been arrested on February 24, 2000, but he cut a deal with the Feds and got off with five years for racketeering. However, he couldn't stay clean on the outside. Even though the judge had said he had "irrevocably broken from his past," he went back to the life of crime. Was he pressured? Was he drawn to the fame? Had he received a threatening phone call? Was it the bull's-eye on his forehead? Who knows?

It made me wonder just how "irrevocable" my break from my past was. Would I get a call? Even worse, what if they threatened Sirarpi? Armando was watching for his chance to take Sammy the Bull out for turning on Gotti. What would he think of me leaving the crime business behind?

There were no secrets inside. I had contacted Jay and told him I needed my file – my legal papers. After the pod leaders got a look at it, word spread fast that I was well connected, but nothing in my file told them about the turn I had made in my life. They just figured that I would be able to figure out a way to drop Sammy the Bull, but I saw him as Salvatore Gravano, a lost soul who needed Jesus.

Suddenly the door clanked open and the detention officer announced, "Munchian. You got a legal visit."

When I entered the conference room, Jay was sitting there with my legal documents spread out in front of him. "Pink handcuffs this time. Maybe next time we should request fur-lined."

"You can see that I'm not laughing."

"Okay. The good news is I was able to get your case reassigned to another judge – Judge Wilson."

"Is he a Christian?"

"I didn't ask. I just know he's not Judge Vernon. As I've been telling you, Vernon is too tight with your prosecutor."

"What about the plea?"

Jay shook his head. "Billie Rosen doesn't plea with the moneymen in drug cartels. She's got all the testimonies from the Fed witnesses and your criminal history with Arizona. And you saw the way Rizzo and Paulette painted the picture. Billie thinks she's got both you and Simen."

"But the Feds couldn't pull enough evidence together to do anything."

"Roger, you're in the state system now, and you got a record here. As far as the system is concerned, you are guilty until proven guiltier. They'll try to break the other yahoos from the cartel, and they'll start testifying and forcing legal briefs, court motions, and hearings to drag this thing out two, maybe three years."

"But with Judge Vernon out, can we get the bond knocked down? I don't want to spend the next three years fighting this case from this zoo." I was thinking of Sirarpi and not being able to hear her voice again.

"No. Billie is already filing motions to delay that. She has a whole warehouse full of red tape that she can pull out any time she wants. Don't torture yourself, Roger. I need you to have your head in the game. You will be ready, won't you?"

Isaiah 40:31 came to my mind: *But those who hope in the LORD will renew their strength. They will soar on wings like eagles; they will run and not grow weary, they will walk and not be faint.*

"I'm ready now."

That night, an intense, cold silence left me with only my thoughts. I recalled the picture of Sirarpi surrounded by purple spring flowers with the white peaks of Mt. Ararat in the background. She was beautiful, with long black hair flowing down her petite frame. Her deep dark eyes came alive in the picture and held my heart captive. Unless Jay could work his magic, I would never hear her voice again. I would never meet her, I would never brush her hair away from her beautiful face, I would never kiss her lips, and I would never wipe a tear from her soft cheeks. Those thoughts tormented me.

A verse from God's Word slowly broke through: *The LORD himself goes before you and will be with you; he will never leave you nor forsake you. Do not be afraid; do not be discouraged* (Deuteronomy 31:8).

My body stopped shivering. Peace and calm covered me, and I fell into a deep sleep.

Chapter 15

Meeting Sirarpi

I had been in county stripes for twenty-one days before Jay finally managed to get the bail dropped to $100,000. I bonded out on April 10, 2000, early enough to call Sirarpi. The conversation didn't start well. A chill came through the line. She didn't ask for an explanation, so I got right to it. I told her that I had been away on business and had no opportunity to call. It was mostly true, I thought. My business had been drugs, and that had called me away.

The state had nailed the entire cartel. Billie Rosen had squeezed all of them. One by one they went down. One by one they told their tales, and as Jay predicted, they painted an ugly picture of me.

The court interview dates with Rizzo and Paulette were set to start in November in Vegas. Jay told me it would be next to impossible to get permission to travel out of state to be there, but he worked his magic, and for the first time in two years, Rizzo and I were in the same room. I think he nearly wet his pants when he saw me. That was also the first time I met Billie Rosen.

Rizzo choked and got his lawyer to have me removed. On the way out, I stared him down and watched him crumble. Same thing with Paulette. Once I was out of the way, Rizzo spewed his rubbish, and court dates mounted.

Sirarpi and I continued our daily conversations. In January, Jay nearly dropped out of his seat when I asked him to file for me to make a trip to Armenia. "Kiddo, do you have any idea what I had to do to get approval for you to cross the state border? How am I going to get Rosen to agree to let her prize fish travel to a third-world country that makes criminal extradition a fifty-year ordeal?"

"Tell them I'm getting married."

"You asked her to marry you?"

"Not yet, but they don't need to know that."

"Are you going to ask her to marry you?"

"I'll know when I get there."

"Did you tell her you're looking at spending the rest of your life in prison?"

"I haven't exactly broached that subject yet."

Jay sighed and said, "I'll see what I can do."

A month later, Jay's voice burst through his office phone full of disbelief. The motion for me to travel had been granted. "You must be back in thirty days for your next court date or your parents can say goodbye to the hundred large they threw in to bail you out of Joe's Happy Hotel."

I spent the next month making arrangements to finally meet Sirarpi. Jay spent the month filing briefs and documents. Two days before I was to fly out, he called me in. "Lazy Su copped a plea. That's the transcript from the interview," he said as he pointed to the tallest pile of papers on his desk. "The picture they're painting is getting uglier and uglier. Her testimony is significant because she worked the closest with you. If this goes to trial, she'll be the hammer that nails your coffin shut."

"Do you really think it will go to trial?"

"I can only drag this out so long. Unless lightning strikes twice, by this time next year we're going to be making trial preparations."

"Lightning strikes twice?"

"We got the hack judge off your case. Now we need a miracle

such as Billie retiring. Otherwise, we get no plea. We're looking at max on all twelve beefs."

My heart sank at that news. "I don't get it. I thought we were ready for this."

"Some cases just don't come together, Roger."

So with a heavy heart, I sat in a plane. In a few minutes we would be up and flying. Phoenix, Arizona, my court case, and Billie Rosen would be more than seven thousand miles behind me. No man is an island. My decisions affect others. I could feel the attack from the Enemy showing me what my past had done and the lives I'd destroyed, and telling me I'd never be able to escape.

My Bible sat on the open tray table in front of me. My spirit stirred as I read Psalm 107:

> *Some sat in darkness, in utter darkness, prisoners suffering in iron chains, because they rebelled against God's commands and despised the plans of the Most High. So he subjected them to bitter labor; they stumbled, and there was no one to help. Then they cried to the LORD in their trouble, and he saved them from their distress. He brought them out of darkness, the utter darkness, and broke away their chains.* (Psalm 107:10-14)

I thought of lost souls who were prisoners in chains: Armando, worshipping with his hooch; Nufo, knocking off his Blockbusters; Martin, my cellmate at Tent City who was drawing a ten-year stretch for trafficking marijuana; and many more. Someone had to share with them that only God could bring them out of darkness. These lost men had to know. They had to know that Christ's love is within reach, that Jesus is real. They may have rebelled, but God's mercies are new every morning. They had to hear that God was reaching out to them with His eternal love.

After the captain's voice announced that we were cleared for takeoff, we flew over Phoenix. I saw the courthouse and the Madison Street Jail. I wondered if that was the last time I would see them – and Billie Rosen.

"Trust Me, Roger. Trust Me."

Yerevan, Armenia
March 2001

The airplane landed on March 5, 2001. My heart leaped into my throat when Sirarpi greeted me as I stepped off the plane. I hugged her and kissed her on the cheek. Then I gently brushed her hair away from her face the way I had been dreaming of. We talked nonstop through the night, then we strolled the streets. I felt so at home. Was it her presence or my Armenian spirit? I didn't know, but I was captivated by the medieval structures, the ancient streets lined with ivy vines, and the gray stone churches with dome tops that reflected the volcanic dome of snowcapped Mt. Ararat in the distance.

I knew I could stay there. I could live there. I would be free. I would be with her. I proposed, and she accepted. We rented a hall at Hotel Yerevan and set the wedding date for March 10 – two days later! Then we headed out to pick out our rings.

"Are you hungry?"

"Hrach, I don't think we've eaten since last night. Yes, I am."

I bought two plates of shish kebabs from a vendor, and Sirarpi and I sat on a ledge by a fountain. Eventually I asked, "Are you really ready for this?"

"I think so."

"Well, listen – there are a couple more things you need to know before we stand before God and vow to share our lives together." I knew she could tell I was deeply troubled.

"Hrach, what is it?"

"First, I've been married before."

Sirarpi's face turned white, and the spark vanished from her eyes.

"She died?"

"Divorced."

"Divorced! She – she left you, right? She's the one who did that to you?"

"No, Sirarpi. It was me."

She started to get up, but I grabbed her arm and gently pulled her back down. "Sirarpi, it was before I came to know God. It was in my previous life."

"But God hates divorce. He says that what He has brought together, let no man pull apart."

"I've struggled with that, Sirarpi, believe me; but take God's complete Word – what God has *brought* together. That marriage was not brought together by God. I know that God is bringing this marriage together. I know it deep in my heart."

"Are there any . . ." she swallowed hard, "any children? Do you have children?"

"No, Sirarpi."

She was silent, thinking about what I had told her. Then she said, "You said there were a couple of things. What else do you want to surprise me with?"

"I have some legal troubles back home."

"What do you mean? Are you a fugitive?"

"I will be if I don't arrive back in the United States by the twenty-fifth. The month that I didn't call you – I only told you a half-truth."

"A half-truth is a full lie, Hrach. Why would you lie to me?"

"My business did cause for me to be away where I could not call you. It was my criminal business. I was in jail."

"Jail?"

"I am out on something called 'bail.' We had to come up with $100,000 cash so I could get out."

"That's a lot of money."

"Yes, and it was money I didn't have, so I had to borrow it from my parents. If I don't come back, they lose their money and I will be a fugitive." I had not yet decided what to do. God was going to have to help me with that. "Sirarpi, I left that life behind when I started pursuing Christ. It was my past. Right now, I can't imagine that future without you."

"Do they always let guys on bail leave the country?"

"No, Sirarpi. It's almost impossible, especially in a case like mine. That's why I'm convinced that God is bringing us together. Only God could make this happen. I'm not promising that this is going to be easy, but I know God has a plan, and I am trusting in Him. This is right, Sirarpi – you and me."

We discussed my previous marriage, the crime case, and the court case, and I insinuated it was no big deal. I only wanted her to be aware of the fact that there were other things going on. I didn't know the future. At that point, we still had a chance. Because the Feds had dismissed my case, I was hopeful that the state would do the same. However, I never told her that I could be facing a life sentence. That would have broken the deal for sure. For more than a year, we had talked on the phone, so she knew me quite well.

Now she was silent. I took her face in my hands and looked into her eyes. "Sirarpi, I know God will see us through. Trust Him."

Her smile slowly returned and warmed me. "We haven't slept in more than three days, Hrach, and we have a lot of work to do to get this wedding together."

I didn't think I could love her any more deeply until that moment. I gratefully and lovingly kissed her, and the world ceased to exist. Tomorrow, God would bring us together as one.

The wedding was beautiful, and the reception was an all-night affair. We fell asleep at the head table while our guests celebrated until dawn.

Sirarpi would not be able to return with me on this trip because her paperwork was still being processed. She had to go through immigration in Moscow. When we arrived at the airport, we were told that I had missed my flight. I wanted this to be a sign from God that I should stay. My court hearing was scheduled for March 29. If I failed to show, it would appear that I had chosen not to go back.

What else could I do now? Zvartnots International was no LAX; it could be a week before the next flight.

"Oh, you're in luck," the attendant said as her fingers worked the keyboard in front of her. "I have room on an Air France flight into Charles de Gaulle Airport, departing here on the twenty-eighth. Then direct to Houston, and a connecting flight with Continental Air should put you in Phoenix by noon on the twenty-ninth."

I was scheduled to be in court at 2 p.m.

"Sir, shall I book this for you?"

He brought them out of darkness, the utter darkness, and broke away their chains (Psalm 107:14).

"Sir?"

"Hrach? What's wrong? The flight. You have to go."

I didn't want to let her go. I could stay. *In their hearts humans plan their course, but the LORD establishes their steps* (Proverbs 16:9).

I knew I had to return Sirarpi to God, and I had to return my own gifts back to God to use for His purpose in reaching the lost and the least.

"Sir?"

"Trust Me, Roger. Trust Me."

"Yes," I said, "book it please."

Chapter 16

A Glimmer of Hope

March 2002

Sirarpi joined me in Phoenix a few months after I returned. We started her immigration process, and five years later, she became a US citizen. She went to church with me, both to Zeke's and to Pablo's, where I interpreted for her. She didn't like the Pentecostal churches. She told me, "I'm going because I'm your wife." From the beginning, she had an issue with their methods. God had given her a sensitive and keen spirit to recognize things for what they were. With her keen intuition, she has been a great complement to me in the ministry. Even though she had issues with the church, she got involved with the ladies there, and that made it better for a time.

As joyful as that time was, though, it was clouded by the knowledge that any day I could be back in court to be sentenced for my activities in Detroit. I had spent my working days building the insurance company that I had begun with my parents, which would provide for the family while I was away.

On March 14, 2002, I was at the Banner Thunderbird Medical Center looking down at my newborn son, Andrew. He was named not only after my father, Andranik, but also in honor of the apostle. The hospital room was quiet. Sirarpi was sound asleep, nestled under the sterile white sheets. She and Andrew would be discharged the next day, and we'd have Andrew home – our home and his home.

I had finally gotten him to sleep. He was at peace sucking on his pacifier. I cradled him in my arms, wanting sleep myself, but not ready to put him in his crib. I just wanted to hold him a little longer. I could never have imagined the level of love I felt for such a fragile, innocent life. I held him, cradled him, and recognized the continued fingerprints of God's infinite love.

I had stopped trying to figure God out. My case was falling apart by the day. I kept the details of my case to myself, but as news got worse and worse, I told Sirarpi bits at a time. She once said, "Learning about you is like peeling an onion. Every peeled-back layer brings more tears." She was not aware of how bad this was, but she continued to find out – one layer at a time.

Jay battled my case day after day. Billie would not budge. Jay did everything he could to negotiate a deal and keep it from going to trial, but Billie knew that her strength was in the courtroom, and she was either going to get me to turn witness or send me off to prison for the rest of my life.

I remembered Isaiah 55:8: *"For my thoughts are not your thoughts, neither are your ways my ways," declares the* LORD. I needed to let God be God, not try to figure Him out. We cannot fathom His ways. Then I read, *Grasp how wide and long and high and deep is the love of Christ, and to know this love that surpasses knowledge – that you may be filled to the measure of all the fullness of God* (Ephesians 3:18-19).

I realized that the only thing we need to figure out is the depth of His love for us. As a father looking down at this young innocence in my arms, I felt the depth of a father's love. I could only imagine the eternal depth of the unconditional love the heavenly Father has for His children.

I knew that I needed to make preparations for prison. Sirarpi needed to be financially secure, so I started the valuation process for Diamondback Insurance. I didn't want to sell the family business, but the initial valuation came back at more than $400,000, and that could provide well for the family for quite a while.

I imagined the dinner table with an empty chair at the head, collecting dust, and my family getting by without the head of the home. Holding Andrew tight, I closed my eyes and prayed:

Father God, you continually convict me with Your Word, reminding me of prisoners suffering in chains, and Your promise to bring them out of darkness. Lord, I pray for Your intervention. I pray that somehow, some way, through Your will and power, that this would not go to trial, that my family will remain whole, and that I can remain with my family and be the husband and father You need me to be. I submit to Your will, though, understanding that You are all-knowing and all-powerful. If the mission field for me is to reach the lost behind bars for the rest of my life, then I accept. I know there are no boundaries to the freedom that comes from Your love. I know that even If I spend the rest of my life here on this earth in prison, I will always remain free in Your love. I accept, Lord, and will serve wherever You need me to be. In Your name, Jesus, I pray. Amen.

A little coo came from Andrew, and then I heard my cell phone vibrate on the table next to my chair. My heart sank when I saw that it was Jay. He never called this late at night with good news. I let it go to voicemail so I didn't disturb Andrew by taking the call. When the voicemail light came on, I put Andrew in his crib and stepped into the hallway to listen to the call.

"Roger," Jay began, "you need to be in court this Thursday, March 21, at two o'clock. Don't miss this one or you'll be back in jail on another half-mil bail. This is our only pretrial hearing. Call me back so I know you got this message. I'm sorry, Roger. I did my best."

I called him back, but he didn't sound very encouraging. In fact, he suggested the unthinkable. "Look, Roger. I can't win this one. You are looking at life, and Rosen is not going to budge. I have another proposition. Take your family – your whole family – and go back to

Armenia. I'll buy your one-way tickets. You can live a normal life as a husband and father and forget this whole mess. What do you say?"

Tears soaked my cheeks. I remembered my prayer, but had to fight the urge to cry out to God: *Why?* Then from inside the hospital room, I heard Andrew cry. Was it colic or did he lose his pacifier? I wiped away my tears and rushed back into the room. My family needed me. They needed a husband and papa.

Thursday, March 21, 2002

Settling into a new routine at home had been stressful. I was headed for work early again before Andrew was awake. Sirarpi was still sitting at the table. She didn't have any more appetite for scrambled eggs than I did. I saw her check my half-eaten eggs and cold coffee, and she mentioned something about me losing weight. I was always preoccupied with everything that was going on.

"I cannot imagine what life would be like without you," she said. "But deep down, I know that I have to face the reality that you could be going away to prison for the rest of your life – for the rest of our lives."

She opened her Bible to Psalm 112:4 and read: *Even in darkness light dawns for the upright.* Then she added, "Those words describe you. Even when darkness sinks around you, there is a brightness surrounding you." Both of us clung to the hope that God wouldn't take me away.

As I left for work, I noticed that Sirarpi was reading another psalm, one that I knew well. It begins, *Whoever dwells in the shelter of the Most High will rest in the shadow of the Almighty. I will say of the Lord, "He is my refuge and my fortress, my God, in whom I trust"* (Psalm 91:1-2).

Neither of us wanted to face the reality that God, a God who is jealous for us, wanted us to completely rely on Him. If I had to leave in order for Him to get Sirarpi's complete trust or my complete trust, He would separate us. That is the one thing we did not want to face.

As I drove to work, I was just routinely going through the motions. I was mentally getting my affairs in order for the trial. I had ignored the morning's edition of the *Arizona Republic*, missing the front-page headline below the fold that read:

Attempt to Kill Prosecutor Fails

Assassination attempt leaves brother wounded

A high-profile Valley drug prosecutor narrowly escaped assassination Thursday night when a bullet fired through a window of her home wounded her brother instead.

The shooting took place shortly before midnight at the north Phoenix home of Billie Rosen, lead drug prosecutor for the State Attorney General's Office, Phoenix police said.

Driving south on I-17, my mind was elsewhere, and the road and world were a fog in front of me. At two o'clock, I would be back in court – only it would be different this time. This time, there would be no hope of a deal with Billie Rosen. There would be no more delays. They would discuss process, jury selection, witness lists, trial dates, and the summation of the charges. It all added up to one thing: life in prison.

He brought them out of darkness, the utter darkness, and broke away their chains. God's Word continued to come back to me. In my fog, I only caught part of the news on the radio:

. . . at this time, the condition of Arizona State Attorney General Prosecutor Billie Rosen's brother is being reported as critical. Phoenix police spokesman Sergeant Anderson said that police are still investigating the incident. Rosen's brother, Richard Rosen, 40, was visiting

Ms. Rosen at the time and reportedly was sitting at a computer in a back bedroom when at least one of four shots struck him.

Investigators believe that a silencer may have been used to muffle the gunshots, which were fired through a screened back window. Anderson said that a crudely made silencer constructed of PVC piping was found at the scene, leading investigators to suspect that the shooter was not a professional killer. No arrests have been made.

I wasn't sure what to make of the report or what it meant until Jay called later that morning. "Did you hear about the incident?" he asked.

"About Billie Rosen? Yeah, just what I heard on the radio."

"Your court date has been cancelled for today. Rosen's schedule has been cleared indefinitely."

"Jay, what happened?"

"Attorney generals like Billie make a lot of enemies, Roger. There is lots of talk about this one being a hit by the Mexican mafia that was planned to implicate you."

"Sounds like what they'd do, but how does this impact my case? What do you mean her schedule has been cleared?"

"Roger, an attempted hit on a ranking counsel with the state AG office is serious business. Investigators are going to be digging deep into every one of her case files in a detailed exam. Who knows – this could be a blessing in disguise."

I didn't deal with the Mexican mafia. Their methods were pretty gruesome. I didn't like street gangs either. They were usually problematic. I preferred working with executive cartels – the guys who wore suits and ties. They were a much better fit for me.

November 2002

I was in the office on a Saturday morning, trying to keep busy – trying to keep my mind off the craziness of my case. I was still in a holding pattern because things were silent at the office of Billie Rosen. I suspected things would get moving again as I sat at my desk and read the story in the *Arizona Republic*:

Two Indicted in Plot to Kill State's Top Drug Prosecutor

Two suspects linked to the Mexican mafia have been indicted in the March assassination attempt against the state's top drug prosecutor.

The conspiracy's central figure, 39-year-old Mark David Branon, was arrested by Phoenix police on Tuesday in connection with the March 2002 assassination attempt on Arizona Assistant Attorney General Billie Rosen.

In 1999, Branon was indicted by a federal grand jury in San Diego and by two Arizona grand juries for overseeing drug rings that smuggled tons of marijuana into the country. While on bail, Branon allegedly contracted the killing of Rosen, who served as the lead prosecutor in Branon's case. The assassination attempt resulted in the shooting of Rosen's brother while inside the Rosen residence. Rosen's brother was severely wounded in the assassination attempt, but has since recovered.

Investigators found a homemade silencer outside Rosen's house. Trevor Alen Rayford, 30, of Phoenix, was indicted for manufacturing or providing the silencer. According to court records, Rayford, known by his street name

"Cool Ray," has at least three prior drug convictions and no previous weapons charges.

In addition to the charges by the state, a federal grand jury also indicted Branon on murder-for-hire charges.

Jay called that afternoon and said, "Rosen's schedule is moving again. She's staying on the case." I suddenly felt sick to my stomach.

He continued, "However, it looks like the AG, Janet Napolitano, is taking her off her high-profile cases. She'll be listed as the lead prosecutor on this case, but she's going after the low-hanging fruit. She'll be prosecuting Gibby and Clay, China Mike and Mo – the ones the AG sees as the lower level of the cartel. Since the AG still considers you top management, your case is being moved to another prosecutor."

"A new prosecutor? Is this rare?"

"Like lightning striking twice in the same spot. But we aren't out of this yet, Roger. This could go either way. We could get a prosecutor willing to deal and keep this out of court, or this assassination attempt could force Napolitano's office to come down harder on drug dealers to send a message that this type of intimidation won't play in the state of Arizona. Let's just look at this as a glimmer of hope that we didn't have before."

Yes, that's what I thought. It was a glimmer of hope – the fingerprints of God.

Chapter 17

Waiting Ends

March 2003

The waiting game never seemed to end, but not wanting to face the possibility of prison, I was thankful for every day that I was free – free to be there for my family, and free to put my life back together.

I had spent the last couple of years confirming my belief that God is real and that the Bible is true. Somewhere during this time, the transformation had happened – being born from above. I discovered some basic facts about the structure of the Bible. For example, it consists of sixty-six separate books. It is not just one big book written by one person. In fact, it was written by about forty different authors throughout about fifteen hundred years on three different continents and in three different languages. That is a miracle in itself, but these books somehow came together in the late first century, pointing to Jesus through prophecy and fulfilled prophecy. It tells of Jesus's accomplishments during the last three years of His short thirty-three-year life. In addition to that, we use His birth year in our calendar system to separate BC from AD.

I knew that Jesus was different from other faith leaders and faith foundations, and I decided that I had enough facts to move forward.

I had been attending Pastor Pablo's Spanish church. I had learned enough about this by reading the Bible for myself, and came to understand that Jesus was this God who not only saved my life from prison, but who even died for me and rose from the grave so that I could have eternal life. What I understood in my head became real in my heart.

So at the age of thirty two, before I was sentenced to do my time on the case from Detroit, I asked Pastor Pablo Contreras to baptize me by immersion. He was shocked because he rarely conducted water baptisms, but he could not refuse my request. None of my family came for the baptism because they really did not understand, and my wife had to stay home to watch the baby, but early one cold morning – at six o'clock – Pablo baptized me. It was just me, Pablo, the water, and God.

Yes, I was loving my freedom and I used it well, but the waiting would soon be over. I was ready – ready to do my time and ready to draw near to God in the confines of the prison cell.

In the meantime, Jay had come up with another proposition. He said, "Look, Roger, I'm not going to win this case. As your attorney, and for the sake of your wife and son, once again my advice to you is to get on a plane and go back to Armenia. It's not too late. Sell everything and go. Start a new life." I could tell he was heartbroken as he looked at my wife and son.

I knew that Pablo and Zeke approved of that proposition, but this was one of the biggest tests of my faith because I was compelled by the Holy Spirit not to run away. I did not have peace with the idea of fleeing to Armenia. It would be selfish to take my wife and son to a world that has terrible health care instead of living where it is the best in the world. Taking them away from the best education the world has to offer to a war-torn third-world country would have imprisoned them. It would have been a very selfish choice. I had to say no. I had to trust God, but it was the hardest decision I've ever had to make – to risk being sent up for life and not being there for my family.

In the end, I had to accept whatever God's will was. Running from God did not work out well for Jonah (as seen in the biblical book of Jonah), and it probably would not work out well for me.

Jay called with the latest news from the attorney general's office. The counsel who had joined the case was a longtime prosecutor named Giovanni. He had a reputation of being old school and tough on drug dealers, but Jay was keeping his ears peeled to the office talk.

"Yes, this guy's been tough on drug dealers, but I heard he doesn't much care for Rosen. He had started playing hardball, but his case-load was swelling with the additional load from Rosen's office. He wants to put as many cases as possible to bed quickly. In fact, he let me know that he is open to negotiation on your case."

"Well, what's it come down to?"

"Giovanni pushed hard to nail you on any of the class 2 felonies, but I wouldn't have it. In the end, I got him to agree to amend Count 12 from 'Transport for sale or transfer of marijuana' to 'Attempted transport.' That reduces it from a class 2 to a class 3 offense – and he dismissed the rest of the charges."

Two days later, the plea agreement was delivered to Jay's office, and I went in and signed it. Seven years flat. I would spend nearly a decade in incarceration away from my family, but I had learned to trust God. As much as it did not make sense to me, I would rather be in God's plan than out of God's plan.

"I will never leave you, Roger. Never."

I sat in my office going through the motions of filing paperwork and cleaning up loose ends. I had just talked to a business broker and asked him to take Diamondback Insurance off the market. Even though I had signed for seven years flat, I wasn't sure the business would make it without me.

I was about to let it go when the marketing rep of one of the companies I worked with walked into the agency. His name was Manny. He was a competent insurance rep looking for new opportunities. After interviewing him, I was sure he had been sent by God. I needed a good agent and manager in order to keep the business, so I hired him, and Manny was able to start right away.

Then my phone rang. It was another call from Jay. "I just got word from the court."

"Yeah?"

"Your sentencing date is April 11, 2003. You need to be in court by 8:30."

I knew that Jay thought I should have fled to Armenia. *He brought them out of darkness, the utter darkness, and broke away their chains.*

"Thanks, Jay," I said.

I hung up, and before I had a chance to think about it, my phone rang again. Sirarpi's sobbing voice came through. "Hrach," she stammered. Her voice was choked with emotion – emotion full of both grief and joy, of the darkness of fear and uncertainty, and of the light of newness.

"Sirarpi, what is it?"

"Oh, Hrach."

"What is it, Sirarpi? What's going on?"

"Hrach, oh, Hrach! I'm pregnant. You're going away, and we're going to have another baby."

Reality hit me. This new child would be getting out of first grade by the time I could hold it for the first time as a free man.

"Trust Me, Roger. Trust Me."

Alhambra State Prison Intake, Phoenix
April 2003

It took longer than half a day because I had several character witnesses who had testified on my behalf on the day of sentencing. Judge Wilson had also received several letters testifying to my new life – a life committed to walking with the Lord – evidence of my newfound commitment to live my life as a contributing member of society and as a family man.

When the judge's decision time came, he said, "Before I sentence you, Mr. Munchian, I want to ask you if you really understand that by delivering drugs and making this substance available on the streets, you're guilty of poisoning thousands of young minds nationwide."

"Yes, your Honor."

"Because it's not really the distribution of drugs that you're guilty of here, Mr. Munchian. If the law allowed me to find the victims, the minds you've destroyed, the futures you've ruined, and the youth you've stolen, I would send you away for multiple lifetimes."

"Yes, your Honor. I understand."

"However, this court listened to the testimony given here today." Judge Wilson referred to himself in the third person, depersonalizing it. That is what judges do right before handing down serious sentences. I couldn't figure out where the judge was going with this. He had signed for seven flat, but judges could always negate a plea. I braced myself for the worst.

"This court has observed you and has listened to the testimonies. There is strength and sincerity about you that cannot be denied. Mr. Munchian, it was the intention of this court to strike this plea and sentence you with the maximum punishment possible for this crime. However, in a rare moment of reconsideration, this court has decided to indeed strike your plea, but to reduce your seven-year sentence to two-and-a-half years in the Arizona Department of Corrections, with a presentence incarceration credit of twenty-one days. Sentence to begin immediately on this date, April 11, 2003."

After the judge's gavel struck the sound block, I was moved to an anteroom. I sat there and waited for them to come and shackle me and load me into the bus. I could not come to grips with what had just happened. The judge had struck my plea – and *reduced* my sentence!

The door opened. An officer came in, handed me a stack of paper-clipped papers, and told me that I was free to leave. The papers were instructions for my self-surrender. My petition for a two-week reprieve to get my affairs in order had been granted. The papers instructed me to show up at the Alhambra State Prison on April 25, 2003, and surrender to state authorities.

It simply did not usually work this way. I should have gone directly from the courtroom into an orange jump suit. It simply didn't happen that someone was sentenced and then given two weeks to get one's affairs in order – two extra weeks with my wife and family. I had to believe that the judge looked at me, a new man, and looked at my pregnant wife and one-year-old son, and God worked in his heart. This was one more miracle to build my faith. The judge had given me the absolute minimum possible, along with two weeks to prepare.

"Trust Me, Roger."

The next two weeks went by quickly. I had to make sure that Sirarpi was able to get her driver's license, and I needed to teach her the business and make sure our financial affairs were in order. Manny would be there to help her, but Sirarpi would be taking over the business for the next two-and-a-half years.

Sirarpi drove me to the Alhambra prison, and I just walked in. It wasn't a normal process where they would handcuff me. My bond was not released until I self-surrendered, and then I got processed. Sirarpi sat on the hard bench and leaned against the cold cinder-block wall. The stench of refuse and ripened filth did not help the nausea of her pregnancy. I had disappeared from her view when the metal doors clanged shut, separating us for what seemed would be forever, even though we would be able to see each other again soon. Another clang startled her. An officer stepped out and said something she did not understand, other than the name "Munchian."

"Me," she said in broken English. "I am Meesus Munchian."

He handed her a plastic bag that contained the clothes I had been wearing when I surrendered that morning. She took the bag, and then the officer handed her a smaller package and said something else she did not understand. He then stepped back behind the threshold, and the door rolled shut.

Sirarpi turned and started to walk toward the door while opening the smaller package. At the bottom of the bag was the ring she had placed on my finger the day we vowed for better or for worse. The ring was soon soaked with her tears, and she ran for the door. She blindly dashed across the street to the parking garage and sat behind the wheel, trying to remember how to work that thing again. She had only been driving for two weeks. I had insisted that she learn because she needed to be able to get around.

Now I was gone. For better or for worse. In sickness and in health. She was alone and had a new life forming inside her – a life knit together by God. She could go back to Armenia where she had family to help her raise her children and where she could speak the language. She would not be so frightened.

However, she had made a vow, and the vow was to God. As frightened as she was, she would trust God. She could tell God how much she trusted Him, but she would also show Him by sticking to her vows.

"Hrach," she said out loud. "Hrach, I love you."

Part 4

God Saves

Chapter 18

Time at Alhambra

I had waved goodbye to Sirarpi before the door slammed shut behind me and the clank of locks echoed in the hall. She was gone. I looked down at the intake papers. Entry date: April 25, 2003. Projected release date: October 7, 2005.

My hands trembled. I was no longer Roger Munchian, a.k.a. Hrach Munchian, a.k.a. Roger Rabbit. I was now inmate #175948. Gender: Male. Height: 66 inches. Weight: 175. Ethnic Origin: Other.

After I had traded my street clothes for an orange jump suit, I was given a sheet of paper that listed my cell phone number. About twenty other inmates were processed with me. We were told to line up in front of a metal door that clanked with a bang and echoed throughout the room. They led us single file into the bowels of the prison. The cell doors shut tightly on lockdown, and once that metal door was shut, the place was as quiet as a library. I found the cell with the numbers that matched the digits on my paper. The door rolled open and the stench of days-old sweat and sewage hit me.

"Inside, Number 175948!"

I stepped past the threshold, and the door rolled shut, sealing me inside the closet-spaced room where two other inmates were sleeping on their bunks, unaware that they had a new roommate. One was a thin guy, no thicker than the rails of his bunk. He reeked from the stench of the streets where he probably spent last night. The other man was wrapped in the cell's only blanket. His gargantuan size was straining the bunk to its limits.

I had no idea what time it was. I only knew that processing had taken an eternity, and I was exhausted. We had no windows to the outside – no sights on descending dusk or a midnight moon. I only knew that it was late. I crawled into the only empty bunk and quickly dozed off to sleep.

A sense that I was being watched woke me. The eyes of an intense dark world startled me when I opened my eyes. The gargantuan who had snapped bedsprings with every breath last night now sat shirtless on the edge of his bunk. He was a bull-chested Chicano. His body was a panoramic, tattooed canvas displaying every symbol of Satan's reign. Across his forehead stretched a gothic 666, and each side of his shaved head was covered in tattooed horns dripping in blood. A fork-tongued interpretation of Satan covered his bald crown. The center of his chest bore a hexagram surrounded by pointed winged representations of Satan's fallen angels whose fork-tailed bodies stretched across his thick shoulders and spilled over onto his back.

Engraved thickly on each of his forearms was an upside-down cross that mocked the crucifixion of Christ, and swastikas dotted into one of his calloused knuckles. Looking into his black eyes was like looking into a cold abyss where deep within, a soul struggled eternally against shackles of hate. He smiled, revealing canines that had been crudely filed into sharp fangs. His nostrils flared as he took in sniff-like breaths like an animal sniffing out its prey – only this animal was not looking to devour meat.

I could not understand the language that he spoke. It was one that I had never heard before, but one that my spirit recognized as the guttural, underworld words with a hellish authority that penetrated my soul like an icicle through my heart. Then he said in a language I understood, "You're a Christian."

I propped myself up on my elbow and said, "Yeah, I am."

"Paul wrote most of the New Testament in prison, didn't he?"

"His letters, yes."

"Persecution. He wrote a lot about persecution, didn't he?"

"That's why he was in prison."

"House arrest. Romans. Wimp."

"So you know the Bible. You know of any way I can get one in here?"

He laughed. "Here? Not a chance, Christian. What do you want a Bible for anyway? The Bible is just a bunch of lies, written by Jews who want to take over the world. They wanted to take the world over back then, and they want to do it now."

"You know, Paul wasn't just under house arrest. Some of his prison time was in dungeons. He was also beaten and left for dead."

"This your first time down?"

"Sort of."

His eyes bore into me. I felt the cold, dark presence of the evil spirit within him. "You look like you only done county time. Yeah, this is your first time on the big-boy yard. You think your God is going down with you?"

"I will never leave you nor forsake you."

"He'll be with me wherever I go."

He chuckled. "If you was God, would you hang out in stink like this?"

"I believe that this is especially where God wants to hang out. This is where the lost are."

"First I was lost, then I was found, sitting in a barbed-wire sewage hole – amazing grace, huh? Okay, so let me tell you how it is here. Get used to this hole. Get used to the smell and stink of bodies from every race God ever thought of. The apes in here are the most rancid. You're sitting in this tiny hole twenty-four hours a day. Every other day we get two hours out; that's it – first to go shower. They cram about twenty of us in the shower room, jammed in a tight line, so get used to it, Christian, and hope you don't get lined up behind some guy who likes it. You're gonna be showering and sleeping stacked up in your cell with all types. Ain't no one been classified here yet, so there ain't no special yards where killers go, where chomos [child molesters] go, where the perverts go. Stripped naked, we all look the same, but you can't mask the soul."

"Lost souls. Only Christ can rescue lost souls."

He smiled with his fangy teeth. "Things are different inside, Christian. Get used to it – if you survive long enough. People watch you. They watch how you walk your walk. Say what you want to say, but how you walk your walk – that's gonna determine if you get out of here either in one piece or cut up in ribbons."

He lifted his pillow and revealed his shank – a crudely sharpened chain link cut from the yard fence. Dropping the pillow back, he said, "I hope your walk is solid, Christian."

I used my isolation time in the cell to talk with God, but I missed having His Word. More than a week had passed, and I had not yet heard about my classification or where I would be sent. I was eager to get to the yard. I craved the sound of Sirarpi's voice. I longed to read God's Word.

After sleeping on the same stained and sweaty sheets for nearly two weeks, I was given a fresh set of linens. When I yanked the dirty ones off, a stack of papers that had been lodged between the wafer-thin mattress and the cement slab fell to the floor. My heart rejoiced when I picked them up and saw torn pages from a Bible. There were four full pages – two from the book of Ezekiel and two from Psalms. The first passage from God's Word that I got to read in more than a week lifted me from the abyss: *I will search for the lost and bring back the strays. I will bind up the injured and strengthen the weak* (Ezekiel 34:16).

I sat down on my bunk and pored through God's Word, devouring each verse the way a starving castaway who had been plucked off a deserted island would devour his first meal.

At 5:30 a.m. the following week, my cell door at Delta pod rolled open. The correction officer's keys jingled on his hip as his huge frame filled the cell door. "Roll up, 175948."

He gave me my classification and informed me of my new address: Arizona State Prison Complex – Lewis, 5-E-6. Building 5, Run E, Bed 6 – or 5 echo 6. I was so relieved when I saw the classification: 3-3. Medium/Maximum security, level 3 – just one tick shy of being tucked away at Buckley unit with murderers and lifers at level 4 – maximum security.

"Trust Me, Roger. Let not your heart be troubled. I am with you."

Chapter 19

Life at Lewis

Stiner Red Yard
Buckeye, Arizona

As our bus rattled through the prison gates of the Arizona State Prison Complex – Lewis, I watched the curly barbed wire glide by. Through the thick glass of the metal door that sealed the inmates off from the air-conditioned cab, I could see the frame of the uniformed driver at the wheel. His back was drenched with sweat, despite the cool air flowing through the wide-open air vents. I sat in the back bolted to a hot metal seat and chained to my seatmate. There was no air conditioning in the back, and the Arizona sun heated the hollow metal tube of a bus to more than 120 degrees.

When the brakes squeaked the bus to a stop, my seatmate and I jolted forward against the metal restraints. Diesel exhaust mingled with the stench of sweat as the driver left the bus idling.

"Welcome to Lewis, ladies! Stiner Red Unit. Get a good look around before you walk in. For most of you, this is going to be the last view of the outside for a long time."

The bright sun made me squint as I stepped from the processing house and pushed my cart loaded with my mattress and orange clothes across the barbed-wire-lined yard. The door to Building 5 was open. As the wheels to my cart bumped over the threshold, I looked down and saw what was being used as the doorstop to keep the iron door wedged open. It was a Bible!

I stooped down and yanked it free. Clutching it to my chest, I quickly jammed my roll of toilet paper under the door to keep it open. I had to give up my toilet paper to get my Bible. It was my only roll of toilet paper for the week, but God was faithful even in here. Another guy had an extra roll, and he gave it to me. That Bible brought a sense of freedom that no chains or metal doors could seal shut.

"I'm with you, Roger. Don't be afraid."

The door to Run E slid open as I pushed my cart across the floor of the semicircular room. I saw the silhouette of a single guard through the circular guardhouse in the middle of the room. Building 5 housed six runs (called jail pods in County) labeled A through F. Thick glass turned each run into a fish aquarium of sorts, each tank stocked with orange piranha searching for prey. The metallic clank and roll of the cell door indicating a fresh fish was like the ringing of a dinner bell.

I left my cart outside and heard the door roll shut as I walked down the aisle of bunks with my mattress slung over my shoulder and with my boots and clothes tucked under my arm. I felt something on my forehead that had crawled out of my mattress, but I didn't dare flinch. I could feel the eyes of hungry predators sizing me up for their next game. I walked on.

I unpacked and settled into my new home within minutes. I stretched out on my bunk, opened the tattered Bible, and started reading. I didn't expect my neighbors to welcome me. It wasn't that kind of neighborhood. Soon the fatigue of the trip overtook me, and I dozed off.

I jumped when I heard my bunk springs creak and felt the bed rattle. A Hispanic youngster sat on the edge of my bed. "Name's Chucky," he said, holding out his hand.

"Roger."

"I run with the Chicanos."

Without asking, I knew what his role was. They were called torpedoes. They were usually chosen from the young ones – kids scared to death by a system that moved them out of the sandbox in juvie and onto the big-boy playground. They'd do anything to feel safe, and that's exactly what the race leaders tasked them to do. Anything – run drugs, call out a snitch, or even drive a shank up through a man's kidney. Chucky's task today was to feel the new guy out and see if he could add him to the Chicano numbers.

I asked, "What time is it?"

"Time don't matter here." He reached down and grabbed a sack. "Got some things here we thought you'd appreciate."

"We?"

"La Raza, Chicanos, homie. It's best you run with us, you know, for protection." He pulled a four-pack of Ivory soap out of the bag. "When you see the skin-dissolver stuff they stock in the showers, you'll appreciate this. Got some shampoo – Pert. Good stuff. The stuff in the showers will rot your head. Some snacks from commissary. There's a few paperbacks in there, but I see you come in with something to read. That don't happen much. Also got a stamped envelope for you. Everyone wants to write to someone right away. Takes time to get money on your books, you know. You can send something out next mail call if you like." He tucked it all back in the bag and handed it to me.

"Thanks."

"What are you readin' man?"

"Bible."

He nodded, with his mind working on his checklist. He was obviously troubled about asking the next question, but he got on with it.

"So what's your story? You know, you tell me, I report it up accurately. If you don't want to share, you're gonna end up talking with the big-stripes anyway because they're gonna ask to see your paperwork. Plus we can't guarantee your safety if we don't know about you."

I was ready for this. This was standard operating procedure. I pulled out my legal papers and handed them to Chucky and his sidekick, Gordo. Gordo looked through the papers. His junior high education was evident by the way he stared incomprehensively at the pages and tried to make out the things he understood.

"Marijuana, huh? Two years on this yard? Man, don't get caught whining. Average rap here is fifteen long."

"I'm just gonna do my time and get out. That's it."

"Okay, so you run with us. We do our meals and rec together. Breakfast is at six, lunch at noon, dinner at five. Get it? You're there whether you're hungry or not. At rec time, you head out to the jungle with us whether you wanna be or not. Think you can do that?"

"I don't exactly have any other plans in my social schedule."

Chucky and Gordo smiled. "Chow is in twenty minutes. Be ready."

In a Routine

More than a month had passed, and I had fallen into a routine. One morning, like every morning, I was up before anyone else on the run. I was sitting on one of the metal stools at the table reading my Bible. For the first three weeks, I used the tattered doorstop Bible until the package arrived from Sirarpi. She had sent me a new NIV Life Application Study Bible just like the one I had outside. I considered this the Cadillac of Bibles. It had many learning tools, such as commentaries, a concordance, a dictionary, references, maps, and so many other tools that were instrumental in teaching me how to apply God's Word to my life.

I read John 14:26: *But the Advocate, the Holy Spirit, whom the Father will send in my name, will teach you all things and will remind you of everything I have said to you.*

I took this verse literally and prayed to my Father in heaven daily to use this Bible to teach me the truth of His Word. I had an unexplainable hunger for God's Word. I knew there were many denominational perspectives and nonessential differences among Christians, and I did not want to rely on human opinions for His teaching. I believed that the Holy Spirit would teach God's truth to me, so I asked with pure motives to know God and His ways like never before. I learned that the eucharist, crossing myself, and worshipping saints were not biblical. Prison was unveiling these things to me and freeing me from the "isms" and traditions of my upbringing and Pentecostal influences. I learned that we are all lost in various systematic, man-made traditions and ceremonies.

At rec, I was required to join the Chicanos when they congregated around their picnic table in the yard to show their numbers. Everything came down to numbers. To the state, I was a number: Inmate 175948. My neighborhood was a number: Building 5. My house was a number: Run E, Bed 6. To God, though, I was not a number: God *knit me together in my mother's womb. . . . I am fearfully and wonderfully made* (Psalm 139:13-14).

Psalm 139:17-18 contained another precious promise: *How precious to me are your thoughts, God! How vast is the sum of them! Were I to count them, they would outnumber the grains of sand.*

My race only thought of me when they needed my numbers. God thought of me nonstop, unconditionally. If I tried to count the number of thoughts God had of me every day, I may as well have tried to count the grains of sand of the earth.

One particular morning I discovered that my race also thought of me when they had other needs. Chucky suddenly appeared and sat down across from me. He said, "Ernie's expecting to meet with you in the *baño* in an hour."

I looked up, trying to figure out what I'd done to Ernie. A summons to the *baño* was an invitation to fight or get beat down. There were no cameras in the john. I'd seen how ugly things could get out of camera range – things such as beatings to the edge of death and near drownings in freshly soiled toilet water.

"It's not for that. Ernie ain't got no beef with you. His area's gonna get a shakedown, and he's holding a pico [knife]. He's gonna hand it to you. Stash it good, maybe in your Bible. You probably won't get hit. If they do hit you and find it, you don't know where it came from, got that?"

The way this kid talked down to me annoyed me. "I've handled my share of weapons in a previous life. No thanks."

Chucky was shocked, unable to comprehend such defiance. "No one's asking you to do a favor. You're being told."

"Who told it?"

"Look, this one's coming all the way from Alejo."

Alejandro, better known as Alejo, was the Chicano race leader for Building 5. The way the hierarchy worked, each run had a leader who reported to the yard leader. The yard leader reported to the building leader. The building leader was closest to the top, answering to the complex leader. Alejandro was like a CEO reporting to the board of directors. "The whole yard's getting hit, man, not just our crib. If you refuse, you're refusing a direct order from Alejo."

"Look, Chucky, tell Ernie I have no problems respecting the politics for the Chicanos on this yard as long as I don't have to compromise my convictions with God. The way I see it, I can choose to obey man or God, and both have consequences; but I prefer a beating from man over displeasing God who has saved me from death numerous times. My witness for Christ is top priority for my life now over my safety." I turned my attention back to my Bible, making it clear that I was done talking.

Chucky called Gordo over. They tried to figure it out, but all Chucky could say was, "You're *loco*, man."

Gordo didn't know what to do. He just sat there. Eventually he said, "Crazy preacher man," and he turned around and left.

I went to the *baño* to tell Ernie, but he was not there. Obviously the news had reached him, and he had picked someone else to do his dirty work. I wasn't sure what to make of it, but I was sure this was not the end of the issue. Most likely, the soap-in-the-socks beating was coming my way one of these nights.

After our show-of-strength meeting in the yard, I hit the running track. Jogging allowed me to be alone with my thoughts while experiencing the freedom of movement within the caged confines of the yard. By the end of the first month, I was up to three miles and had trimmed down to the weight of my high school football days. Before hitting the track, I would pick a Bible verse and meditate on it nonstop, every lap. By doing this, I would memorize one or two verses every day. The peace of the Holy Spirit encompassed me like never before. By my third month, I was up to five miles a day.

I was usually alone on the track, but one day I sensed the presence of someone else. As I ran, I heard the pounding of feet crunching the gravel behind me and gaining on me. I continued to run steady until I rounded the first leg, and with the sun behind me, I noticed not one, but two pursuers gaining on me. I thought of Ernie and the pico and figured my time had come. Two months had passed since that incident. He didn't lose the knife, but I still expected my name to be added to the list.

I stepped up my pace without looking back, but they closed in fast. Just as I was about to cut and run from the track, they drew alongside me, one on each side, both winded and hacking. Neither one was conditioned for the brutality of jogging in work boots.

"You wanna slow it down for us a bit, bro?"

Both were from my Chicano race and were high up in the pecking order. Sanchez and Torres were from Run A and hung close to Alejandro. I slowed down just a little, but didn't stop running.

"Alejo, he's been watching you close, over a month now, right?" Sanchez huffed. "Okay, so now Alejo's ready to meet the new fish."

I kept jogging, not answering.

Torres said, "He wants to meet the preacher man."

That stopped me. Both Torres and Sanchez bent over with their hands on their knees, coughing and gasping for air.

"Preacher?"

"Yeah, yeah," Torres said. "That's what he's calling you. Preacher Man. When Alejo tags you with a name, it sticks with you. You keep it. You ain't got no choice, nope."

"I kind of like it."

"That's good," Sanchez said, "because now it's yours. You got an invite to the head table tonight, Preach. No RSVP required. See you there."

I showed up. Alejo's face was wind-burned and ruddy. His brown skin was grayed by a life sentence in the jailhouse air. Alejandro could have been a Latino movie star if he had chosen a different path. But gangbanging led to drugs, drugs led to murder, and murder led to a life sentence in prison. He had a reputation on the street of always packing two, but only needing one and using one: one gun, one bullet. He had put eleven guys down until he hit a cop's son, which brought the heat down on him hard. He had spent most of the last twenty years up on the max yard. Now he was a lifer on a medium security yard, with two hours out, twenty-two locked down. That's the best he would ever hope for throughout the rest of his life.

"I ran a make on you, and your paperwork looks clean, Preach," he said, taking a long drag off the coffin nail. "You ain't a snitch, at least I don't see it or smell it. You was all cliqued up with some serious movers. You been out of commission for a while, from what I gathered. Trying to walk it straight. But straight don't cut it for guys like us, huh, Preach? Past catches up with us, huh?"

"I made my mistakes. Now I'm paying for them."

Alejandro flicked a long ash into the coffee cup he was using as an ashtray. He glared at me for a long time through stone-cold eyes. "What kind of debt you gotta settle on the outside?"

"What makes you think I'm still looking over my shoulder?"

"You got told. You dissed us, Preach. I need to know why you done that. It takes real brass to pull something like that. Makes me think I'm dealing with someone who ain't afraid of getting smashed in here, as if someone with some backing is gonna come in and bite ol' Alejandro and his homies if we try to issue some discipline."

"As a dog returns to its vomit, so fools repeat their folly."

"Come again?"

"It's a proverb."

"What's it mean?"

"It means I don't go near drugs. I stay away from them. If it means I get smashed, I get smashed. I only have the Lord to back me. That's it."

Alejandro dropped his cigarette butt into the coffee cup and shoved his snacks aside. "I've been in this joint nearly twenty years, Preach," he said. "I see a lot of your type come in here. They find God on the way in and pray themselves to sleep at night. But it's one thing to talk it in here, and another to walk it. I watch the jailhouse preachers melt right into the sludge that surrounds them. These bars kill a man's soul. They'll still talk the talk, but then you see them juicing their veins in the *baño* or scorin' hooch from under a toilet. Half the guys I put down in this joint were jailhouse preachers in hock for the gambling holes they dug themselves into supporting their habits."

"So why are you telling me all this? Why single me out?"

"My eyes have been on you, Preach. I've been watching real close. I've been pretty impressed by what I see so far. If ever the real deal comes through here, it would be you. That's why I decided to look the other way with this Ernie thing. But one step left or right from you, and I'm gonna have to reevaluate things. Do we understand each other?"

"I think so."

Alejandro leaned forward. "Okay, so here's the next favor I'm going to do for you. There's likely gonna be a riot in here tomorrow night around chow time. Tension's been brewing between the Woods [Whites] and Brothers [Blacks] over some gambling debt. It ain't our beef, but if this thing blows, this whole cafeteria's gonna be banging. If you don't join in, Chicanos gotta put you down. If this happens, I know it's gonna go against your preacher walk. I'm telling you, hang back. Fall back behind the crowd. Be ready to go if your homies need you, but you hang back. You're still supporting us, but you just got less risk getting pulled into the mix-up. You got that?"

"Yeah, I think I get the picture, but something tells me you got something else on your mind."

"Yeah. You preacher types like to do your preaching to anyone who wants to listen. We're all square as long as you stick to your race."

I was tempted to argue, to let him know that the Word of God knew no skin color and was not restricted by racial boundaries, but I knew I had a narrow thread to weave here. I had to work within the politics and respect of the system.

"I'll be mindful." I got to my feet and started to leave.

"Let's hope so. It's a rare thing to get a meeting with Alejandro and walk away from him in one piece. Let's hope there ain't gotta be another meeting."

"I'm sure there won't be."

I had been preaching and teaching on the yard, so my reputation was getting around. Guys would ask me questions, and I would answer, and soon more would hang around me. This often turned into two different study groups – one in English and one in Spanish. God was creating the ministry in me and through me without me having any formal schooling or authority. He was preparing me for the ministry on the outside that would serve those on the inside, and individuals living in other parts of the world.

Tension was thick the following night at chow. The correctional officers must have sensed that something was going down or had picked up the rumor that a score was about to be settled between the Woods and the Brothers because they had doubled their numbers. I had barely touched my food when Gordo suddenly slid his tray on the table and plopped down beside me.

"The big-stripes are still negotiating. They got their torpedoes moving back and forth between the tables. If they don't make nice in about fifteen minutes, the place is gonna blow. We got a wager going on you. Have you heard about that?"

"No."

"Whether or not you hang back or mix it up. We know Alejo gave you the okay to hang back, but in here, when things start flying, everyone's tempted to smash a Brother or two, you know?"

"Where'd you put your money?"

"That you bang."

"You didn't choose wisely."

"I think that I may have. I got information you don't have. Alejo knew all about it too."

"What's that?"

Gordo pointed over to the table of Brothers, and my heart sank when I recognized the short guy on the end, the one with the slant to his eyes.

Gordo said, "China Mike. He just came in. Alejo knew he was on his way a few days ago before he hit the yard. What do you think now? If the place breaks out, all hell will break loose and give you a chance, huh? A chance to put down the guy who witnessed against you – the guy who helped put you here. Yeah, you still got that killer instinct, Preach. Yeah, I think I made the right bet."

I had never met China Mike before, and I wasn't sure if he testified against me or not, but I knew I had to pray for him and hope things didn't get ugly between us.

Chapter 20

Times of Testing

Buckeye, Arizona
December 2003

The chain link fencing and grey block watchtowers rising above the compound turned the majestic Arizona mountain ranges into an ugly thing. Visitation was on Saturdays. Once a week I had six full hours to spend with my family. Andrew always grew excited as they neared the prison.

Sirarpi told me that he always shouted, "Papa's house! Papa's house!"

Such childlike enthusiasm. Yes, Lewis State Prison – with sealed gates, colorless buildings, and fences – was my house. The orange garb that stripped away my identity had no effect on a one-year-old boy. Once a week with me, his papa, was so much fun. Orange pajamas didn't matter to him.

Rachel was almost a month old already and was learning to coo. My mama always rode in the backseat with the children and played along with their excitement. She would say, "Yes, Papa! We're going to see Papa soon!"

Sirarpi told me that she wished their childlike faith was contagious. Instead, she looked at the ugly complex and thought of the time stolen from her and of the husband who had been taken from her. She thought of the lonely nights and the empty chair at the dinner table. She wanted the security of a God-fearing husband at her side. Instead, it was stolen time – time that could never be returned.

Sirarpi even told me about the loneliness she felt in the church. She felt like an outcast. She got sympathetic smiles and clammy handshakes, but they forgot her after the services were over. I suggested that maybe they did not know how to deal with the wife of a felon. No matter what, Sirarpi said she sat in the pew surrounded by the "body of Christ," yet felt abandoned and alone.

We both looked forward to that visitation time together. Sirarpi said, "I cherish this time to witness the joy and peace that has settled upon you with an inexplicable reverence. You have a glow – a deep peace that I know comes from intimacy in using this time to draw close to God." *Come near to God and he will come near to you* (James 4:8).

Every week when our time was over, Sirarpi would look back at me and wave goodbye; then the iron doors would slam shut. Our goodbyes were tear-filled, but I always returned to my cell with peace in my heart. I knew I was going back inside to spend countless precious hours alone – with God.

I knew that Sirarpi felt as though she were the one in chains. This feeling allowed her impossible circumstances to imprison her more than if she had been locked inside the walls of the Lewis prison. She was trying to understand. I asked her to meditate on Isaiah 55:8-9: "*For my thoughts are not your thoughts, neither are your ways my ways,*" declares the LORD. "*As the heavens are higher than the earth, so are my ways higher than your ways and my thoughts than your thoughts.*"

"What does that mean, Hrach?" she asked.

"It means to let God be God."

God had not only removed everything that I depended on, but He also removed everything that Sirarpi had relied upon in order for her to learn to trust and completely rely on Him. In simple words, God was saying, "Don't ask Me why. Just trust Me and the plans I have for you."

Sirarpi then told me, "I will start to ask God *what* He wants me to do instead of asking Him *why*. I will trust His promise in Jeremiah 33:3: *Call to me and I will answer you and tell you great and unsearchable things you do not know.* I will let go and let God be God."

The expected chow-hall riot between the Woods and the Brothers never went down, but I knew that Alejandro continued to watch me and wait for my reaction to China Mike. In his world, if a guy helps put you away, you put him down. I lost my chance with the freebie. A chow-hall mix-up would have allowed me that opportunity. However, I knew it wasn't a revenge line that I would have crossed, but it would have been the race line. Rather than reaching out with a fist in revenge, I would reach out in love with God's Word.

My first encounter with China Mike came two days later during free time, which we called "rec." China Mike was strangely alone, isolated, sitting at the only picnic table with an obstructed view of the tower, which made me wonder if it hadn't been arranged. Was Alejandro pulling some strings to get the guy alone so he could watch to see what the Preacher Man would do? I was walking a tightrope, fully aware of hidden eyes on me as I approached China Mike from behind. I kept it simple, pushing the race line and crossing just enough for Mike to get the message.

"Hi, Mike."

He looked up and his slanted eyes widened in recognition. He didn't know what to say. His eyes darted back and forth. He suddenly realized that he was alone. His mouth moved, but he was not sure what I was up to.

"God loves you, brother." I reached out with a brotherly handshake and patted him on the back. Then I moved on. Message delivered. Seed planted: God loves you.

Sometimes that's all it took, but I had dissed my race and was out of line. However, I refused to sweat the consequences. God told us in 2 Timothy 1:7 that *the Spirit God gave us does not make us timid* [fearful], *but gives us power, love and self-discipline.* The Holy Spirit was not merely counseling me and teaching me the truth of God's

Word, but He was living inside me. I could have the same power that resurrected Christ from the dead. I refused to sit idle as a Christian in name only. I had spent the first twenty-five years of my life idle. Coming from a "Christian" country had earned me the Christian title by heritage, but not by the sacrificial blood of Christ.

Like many others, I had been labeled a Christian at birth according to my heritage. My parents had slapped a "Christian" label on my forehead when I was born and had me baptized as an infant, so all my life I assumed I was a Christian, yet I never understood what I believed. I was never a true born-again believer. I had no clue what it meant to be a Christian. This happens to every human on earth. As soon as they are born, someone slaps a religious label on them. We all have the same problem. That label from birth had not made me a Christian, and such a label cannot make anyone else a Christian. Becoming a Christian only happens when we place our total trust in Jesus Christ for salvation.

I was surrounded not only by depraved and wicked hearts, the worst of the worst, those who were ready to pounce at my first misstep, but more importantly, I was surrounded by contrite and broken hearts that were seeking hope and light in a wickedly dark place. I was really no better than they were, so how could I judge them?

My Damascus moment had come at dawn when the light of Jesus Christ lit a dark jail cell. Dusk had begun to settle as God allowed my past life to catch up with me. Darkness came in the encroaching shadows of the chain-link prison yard, but it was in the midst of the darkness, in the midst of the hurting, the lost, and the helplessness, that I recognized the power and majesty of the light of Jesus Christ shining through me. In this place of constant lockdown, prison politics, and twenty-four-hour surveillance by correctional officers and race leaders, I knew that I could not afford to hide that glorious light. There were too many lost souls, too many people who were hopeless and helpless. I understood the words of Jesus to the apostle Paul as applying to me:

Now get up and stand on your feet. I have appeared to
you to appoint you as a servant and as a witness of what
you have seen and will see of me. I will rescue you from
your own people and from the Gentiles [or, inmates]. *I*
am sending you to them to open their eyes and turn them
from darkness to light, and from the power of Satan to
God, so that they may receive forgiveness of sins and
a place among those who are sanctified by faith in me.
(Acts 26:16-18)

I had just dozed off after morning chow when the door chambers rolled and the door slid open. Over the intercom, the officer started calling out the fortunate names who had visitors.

"Munchian, bed six!"

I popped up from my bunk, grabbed my Bible, and fell in line, eager to see my family. I was excited to share some good news with Sirarpi. The metal door to the visitation room slid open, and I saw Sirarpi and Mama sitting at the table. My dad wasn't there, but that didn't surprise me. It was difficult for him to see me locked up, so his visits were very few and far between. Andrew looked up from ramming his Hot Wheels car across the Formica table. His eyes lit up, and he ran to me and leaped into my arms. "Papa! Papa!"

Sirarpi's eyes sparkled as I approached. I held Andrew with one arm as he clung to my neck. Rachel was asleep in her car seat. Mama smiled with the love and warmth of a mother. Today was special. Today Andrew let me be the Shelby and he was the black car. At one point, he made a sound of screeching car tires and an explosion with his lips as he spun the car into a metal chair leg. The black car bounced off the chair leg and tumbled across the floor.

Immediately I felt the tightening of the seatbelt around my chest and the suffocation of the airbag. I saw the white-hot explosion in my mind, and I heard the haunting cries of life being whisked away into the night. It all felt real again.

"Hrach? Hrach?" Sirarpi gently touched my shoulder. "Mama, he's burning up."

I saw the drop of sweat fall from my forehead and splash in front of the tiny car. My fingers clenched the tiny car until they turned white.

"I forgive you, Roger. Let it go."

A calm swept over me, and a peace beyond anything I could understand filled me. I looked up and saw that Andrew continued roaring the black car along the floor, unaware of the moment Papa just had.

"I'm okay, honey," I said. "Just a memory." I noticed the concerned look on Mama's face and gave her a reassuring smile.

"Let's visit a little," I said as I parked the Shelby by the other toy cars. Sirarpi and I walked outside to sit at a table in the smoking area so we could have some privacy. We talked for more than an hour about everything from housekeeping issues to God and our growing faith. We shared Scripture together. I led, and Sirarpi listened intently. I noticed the way her faith grew stronger, and I admired her more and more.

I flipped to Matthew 25:40 and read: *"The King will reply, 'Truly I tell you, whatever you did for one of the least of these brothers and sisters of mine, you did for me.'"* I was about to comment on that when I noticed that Sirarpi's expression seemed distant.

"Aren't we the least of these, Hrach?" she asked.

I paused, and then I looked in her eyes and saw a pool of tears magnifying a deep-down hurt that only the love of Christ could reach. "You're still not going to church?" I asked.

She shook her head and looked down. "No, Roger. I just can't. I can't sit in that pew anymore and pretend that everything is fine. I feel like I just don't belong there."

"You need to worship, though. It's part of getting to know Christ better. Worship."

"What about your worship here, Hrach? Where is your worship in here? Where's your church?"

I looked around the room and saw faces of the dejected. They were dressed in orange and had joyless expressions. All the faces seemed the same. Worry lines creased their paleness, and their eyes were deep with the eternal thoughts that come with long, empty days. Smiles could be forced and could be made to appear as genuine as those on any Hollywood actor, but the eyes were windows to the soul and revealed the truth. The souls behind these eyes were seeking an ear to listen to them or a compassionate voice to reassure them that they were still human.

Through those windows, I could see the tiny flames deep down in each of them. Only the fuel from the sacrificial blood of Jesus Christ could ignite an eternal flame that could never be extinguished – even in this den of hopelessness. These people needed to be reached. They needed to know the eternal hope of Jesus Christ.

Where was the church? I saw the chaplain once and asked him why we don't have church services on Stiner Red Unit. He just shrugged his shoulders and said he had no volunteers willing to come out during the times available for services. Where was the bigger church? In a place of such ripe harvest, where were the faithful who were willing to draw close and bring the light of Jesus Christ?

"I'll write another letter to the pastor," I said. "Many times we helped him make mortgage payments to keep the church doors open. We gave a lot of money."

Sirarpi shook her head. "No, Hrach. No more letters. They just don't know what to do with us."

I recalled that when Pastor Zeke was down and out, he would come to us and ask for more money. We would help him out, just trying to be a good Christian family, but he had not responded to my letters or returned my wife's calls. Our hearts broke when Sirarpi needed support, but they were too busy to help her. She was very disappointed. This was my second experience of heartbreak in a church. I reminded my wife that we should not assume that all people who call themselves Christians are perfect or are representative of the truth of Christ. Sometimes the church's ways compromise the very standard of the Bible's teachings and precepts.

"Things are going to get better, Sirarpi, I promise. I have some good news." I saw her perk up immediately. "I just got reclassified. I'm being moved to a medium-security yard. Probably Bachman Yard."

"Oh, praise God! How? I thought you said you'd be here for the rest of your time."

That was true. After my six-month reclassification, I didn't expect to be reclassified at all. At best, I would be moved from a 3-3 to a 3-2, but one more "unheard of" thing happened. Two weeks after my reclassification meeting, I received formal notice that I was now a 2-2. I would be getting my orders soon for my move to a medium-security yard.

I told Sirarpi, "It's all God. All God. Listen – about Bachman, I get two visits a week – Saturday and Sunday. Also, I hear that Del, a retired brother who walks with a cane, comes in on Monday nights to conduct Christian church services."

"Praise God!" Her eyes filled with tears. "When do you get rounded up, Hrach?"

I laughed. "Rolled up, Sirarpi, rolled up. I expect it will be in a month or so – at least by mid-January."

When visiting hours were over, I walked with my family as far as I could. I kissed my mama before she ushered the kids through the maze of metal detectors and uniformed guards. Then I took Sirarpi aside. "Sirarpi, even Jesus was held in jail as He faced a capital case. He used His time of suffering to get closer to His Father and fulfill His Father's will."

"Hrach?"

"He showed us the way. Jesus came here and was beaten and rejected. The anguish He experienced brought Him closer to God, even to the point of sweating blood at the thought of becoming separated from His Father. Sirarpi, you don't have to be in chains. This time of trial may be the only time you will ever have to experience this intimacy with God that can be deeper than you could ever imagine. Join me on this journey, Sirarpi. Join me. We may not realize it now, but this may be one of the best things that happens to us – a blessing in disguise!"

A tiny flame of understanding flickered through her tears that cast a light on her soul that had been suddenly released from the bondage of worry. My heart practically burst with a new level of love for her that I had never felt before. It was a love that I would not have recognized outside these walls.

"I love you, Hrach. I love you so much."

"I love you more."

Another Meeting with Alejo

In another meeting with me, Alejandro said, "You got powerful friends on the outside, don't you, Preach?" I had expected the meeting. The news spread fast that Preacher Man had skipped an unprecedented five classifications.

"I have only one powerful friend, Alejo. I'd be happy to introduce Him to you. There isn't any politics with Him. He doesn't look at skin color. He doesn't care what race you run with or where you fit in the pecking order."

"Yeah, I know, I know, Preach. Jesus Christ."

"He's the only powerful friend you'll ever need, Alejo. I never realized Jesus was all I needed until Jesus was all I had. I pray that someday you'll grasp that powerful reality."

"Good luck to you, Preach. Don't expect no going away party."

Chapter 21

The Hostage Standoff

January 18, 2004

I knew Sirarpi was excited about my move and was anxious to hear from me that I had rolled up and moved to the medium-security yard. She was well aware of how dangerous it was for me on Stiner Red. I know she had hoped to find peace and freedom in the United States, because she had grown up with bombs, bullets, blood, and death on the streets of Armenia. America was supposed to be different, but she learned that blood was shed here as well.

She now knew about the Aryan Nation, Bloods, and Crips. They ran the streets where I grew up like the soldiers ran the streets of Armenia. I had gained street smarts that gave me an innate sense of survival, but she worried that those senses may have dulled, so she waited for the day that I would be moved.

She flipped on the TV one particular morning for the news and screamed at the first story. Mama heard from the kitchen and dropped her coffee cup, which shattered into pieces.

"No! No! Oh, Hrach – no!"

She didn't understand all the words that the news anchor said, but she knew something had gone wrong at Lewis prison – very wrong.

I had figured this would be the day. I expected the order to roll up to hit the medium-security yard would be given to me by noon. Instead, I woke to find that no one was going anywhere. The entire prison was on security lockdown. This meant that we were locked down in a hole twenty-four-seven with twenty incarcerated men whose only glimpse of freedom was the short two hours out on the caged yard.

Gone – gone was the possibility of rolling up and moving on. Tension would soon be running thick, and tempers would be short.

Lockdown on the yard was the final yank of freedom short of being put in the hole. Freedom was marked by clicks on the clock. Two hours out, twenty-two locked inside. Two hours of freedom, one hundred and twenty ticks, was all we had in the joint, unless, of course, one finds real freedom in God's Word.

Lockdown meant no commissary – no store – which meant no sugary treats and no salty snacks. It also meant no cigarettes. For many, nicotine was just as much barter for goods as it was nectar for life. Chow hall was cancelled. Instead, meals of stale sandwiches were served in brown paper sacks.

The only thing that lockdown didn't stop was the flow of information. The officers could lock the joint down airtight, but the brick walls remained as porous as sponges. Within two hours, the word was out. Two cons over on Morey Yard – a lifer named Steven Coy and a big-stripe named Ricky Wassenaar – jacked the gun tower and took hostages. One hostage, who had only been on duty for three weeks, was blazed with Wassenaar's shank and taken out of commission. The other badge was a female, and Coy and Wassenaar had her in the pen all to themselves, with assault rifles at the ready to keep the heavily armed officers and deputies at bay.

The first day passed with an eager anticipation that this would be over soon. We thought that the two cons up there would run from the tower, escape through the administration building, and turn up as coyote fodder in the desert; or this would end with both of them on the tower floor with a sniper bullet in the head. I was disappointed that the anticipation was not one of compassion for the hostages or for the two fellow inmates, but the general desire was a selfish one to end the lockdown and get the few clicks of freedom back.

Information about the standoff leaked in daily. During brown-bag dinner on day three, Gordo shared the latest. "Okay, so word up on Coy," he said, pulling his sandwich from the bag. "He played Wassenaar on this whole thing."

"What do you mean?" asked Smith, another Christian inmate in my echo run. He was a white guy running with the Chicanos on this day because race restrictions had been relaxed during lockdown.

"Okay. So a while back, an eighteen-year-old fish came in fresh after spending the last four years as a guest wearing the yellow shoulder stripes for Uncle Joe."

I knew he was referring to a juvie who had spent the last four years in the Maricopa County Jail on an adult beef. The hard-core juvies didn't go to State wearing the tan sweaters and brown slacks. They served hard juvie time as guests of Sheriff Joe, wearing prison stripes and pink underwear. The juvie shirts were marked by yellow shoulders.

"A trusty wolfhound at reception targeted him. The trusty has earned his good time by brokering mules for all races except the Chiefs."

The wolf-pack mentality broke my heart more than anything – targeting the young kids coming into the adult system out of juvie. No matter how hard core their reputation on the outside was or how much time in the Maricopa hole had hardened them, they all hit the yard as young boys, fresh and terrified, entering a world of adult predators. I wished there was a way to reach them before they got to the yard – before they recycled one too many times through the juvenile system and ended up here.

God, show me the way. Show me how.

I knew that once you hit the block, your options were limited. You would get targeted that moment by a well-connected trusty or a long-timer looking to make points with some big-stripe matching his race. You will mule and mule hard, targeting whomever they tell you to target, hitting whomever they tell you to hit, and pushing whomever they tell you to push; otherwise, you would join the yard queens or get a false beef tagged to your paperwork that would eventually get you shanked or would result in a series of unwelcomed visits in the *baño*. No matter how you ranked in the juvie, you'd be a sewer rat here.

Unless you find God, the road gets ugly. Without a walk with Christ, you will eventually get used to your role as a torpedo for the crew chiefs. It becomes your lifestyle – muling, stabbing, killing, cleaning up the hit list. You're not allowed to think for yourself. They turn you into what they need – a real hard-core torpedo, seasoned and valuable to the big-stripes and your benefactors. That is how Stiner Red earned the nickname "Stick-em Stiner."

You might be eight years down on a ten-year beef, with two more to go down the road until your journey would be over; but your last drop might go bad and you get caught in prison politics. Like a good soldier, you take the fall and your dime turns into a life term, even though you feel you've earned enough stripes to walk away and do the rest of your time easy.

Your benefactors smile and say, "Sure, enjoy your life." Two weeks later, you're beat into a coma. Waking up in the infirmary, you realize that staying in got you a life sentence, but getting out would be a death sentence. For the first time, you look back on it and realize the true hopeless abyss your life has become.

At the end of the line, there's a prison graveyard or family plot with the unanswerable questions: Why? Where did it all go wrong?

I knew it all went wrong for me without Christ. I had to believe there was a way to reach these young kids with the truth of God's love before it was too late.

Gordo continued. "The fish didn't bite. In fact, he dissed the trusty all wrong. So the guy made arrangements for the kid to get sent up the road with some bad beef on his file. Magically, the kid finds himself on Main Street, not fish row where he was supposed to go, and he's on the yard alone. No one wants him. The kid's jammed up and the word is out that he's narced on some Big Homie – Mexican Mafia – and the eMe put the green light on him. The wolf pack started moving on him one morning, and that's when Coy stepped in. The officers ended up calling it a day for the kid. He got put in protective custody, and Coy got put on the eMe hit list. Coy's been trying to either get checked into PC himself or get taken off the yard, but the officers have been playing hard nose with him. They know what happened. Coy saved them from having a dead fish on their yard, and they thank him by jamming up his case. That's the way the system works, man."

"So how'd he play Wassenaar?" Smith asked.

"Wassenaar's been a rabbit since he hit the yard. You know. Someone's always talking about giving himself a permanent furlough. Word up is that Coy knew this thing would go bad, but as long as he could keep a sniper's bullet out of his bean, playing this thing out with Wassenaar could get him off the yard, maybe even transferred to another prison."

Smith said, "Once you're on the eMe list, they can find you anywhere."

"It's the best chance he's got."

The days dragged on and tempers rose. There was no laundry duty, so the peels ripened daily with the stench of body odor and jailhouse sludge. The officers finally allowed the inmates to fire up their TVs, and the run was allowed to watch the hostage standoff filtered through the eyes of the news cameras like the rest of the world.

As I watched the TV, I felt the convergence of two worlds – two lost worlds. There was a barbed wire world inside gray walls, and there was another world that was free of chains and razor wire, but was shackled in selfish pursuit and worry.

The well-groomed reporters stood outside the prison and lent their expertise on the situation inside the walls. They babbled on about the barbaric inmates, and they dehumanized the entire prison population with their rhetoric. I suddenly felt an unexpected wave of compassion for both the hostages and the inmates. There was no concern around me for the innocent lives at risk up there or for the two men. They only cared about getting out of lockdown. They wanted their store, their smokes, and an hour of freedom in the yard.

Outside the prison, people watched the news with indifference. The networks got their ratings, and the audience got their fix. I had to wonder, though, if the prisoners got their prayers. Their barbaric act deserved the outrage I felt, but why was I feeling this sudden compassion? The Holy Spirit reminded me:

> *When he saw the crowds, he had compassion on them, because they were harassed and helpless, like sheep without a shepherd. Then he said to his disciples, "The harvest is plentiful but the workers are few. Ask the Lord of the harvest, therefore, to send out workers into his harvest field."* (Matthew 9:36-38)

I had to wonder how many Christians sat in their living rooms and watched these events unfold, oblivious to the rich harvest behind the gray walls. How many were moved to pray? How many cared to join the few workers who were trying to reach the lost and helpless behind these bars?

Is the church afraid to apply Matthew 25:31-46? Are they simply overlooking this Scripture passage where God separates the sheep from the goats and demands that the sheep (true Christians) and goats (false Christians) visit the prisoners and the sick, give a drink to the thirsty, feed the hungry, and invite the stranger in? Is God using these missions to test the hearts of the churches, to determine who goes to hell and who goes to heaven? The way the church responds to the opportunities God provides for reaching the least of these in their communities is an indication of the condition of their hearts.

Considering my own church's response to my wife and family, I had to believe that not many were moved to help. Every day, the burden for the whole harvest of those who were Christians in name only grew in me. Their hearts needed to be turned. They had to be found and brought to God.

The hostage standoff lasted two weeks. On Super Bowl Sunday, February 1, 2004, while the world watched the New England Patriots beat the Philadelphia Eagles, a deal was reached. Wassenaar and Coy descended the gun-tower stairs with their hostages and turned themselves in to the FBI negotiators who granted them what inmate Coy had been seeking all along. Coy not only got removed from the yard, but he was eventually transferred to a state prison back east, closer to his family.

Two weeks later, I got the order to roll up. It was after midnight when the captain clanged his baton on the footrail of my bunk and told me it was time to go. I bundled my things and walked through the maximum-security doors for the last time. A quiet desert chill settled in through my peels as I stepped through the same door where I had found the Bible jammed as a doorstop just less than a year ago.

In the distance, I could see the Morey Yard gun tower where the inmates had hunkered down with their hostages. The metal doors of Stiner Red slammed shut, and I sensed that there had been a purpose for my time here. The quiet Spirit of Jesus Christ had moved in me. I knew that the nine months of my undivided attention to God and His Word had prepared me for the next part of my mission – the mission within the harvest-rich confines of the prison yards.

Chapter 22

Released and Ready

December 9, 2004

I had finished serving my time in the medium-security prison. The baggy, state-issued blue jeans hung on my narrow waist and itched horribly, but they matched my denim shirt that was two sizes too big. It felt good to be wearing something other than my orange peels as I sat on the bench in the processing room. I watched the clock. In twelve minutes, the metal door would roll open and I would walk out into freedom. I had twelve minutes to think about the last couple of years.

God used the strict confines of the maximum-security yard on Stiner to hold me close and allow the Holy Spirit to teach me and give me His vision. The confines of that yard allowed me to grow in the Word of God and increase in spiritual maturity. God's promise in Proverbs 3:5-6 sustained me: *Trust in the LORD with all your heart and lean not on your own understanding; in all your ways submit to him, and he will make your paths straight.*

Then God released me to the medium-security yard of Bachman where I had just enough freedom to start making His vision for my life a reality. Prison politics were still around me, but medium security meant that prisoners only had three to four years left. Everyone was too concerned with doing the rest of their time easy and trying not to get caught up in the power struggle of the prison politics. Besides, the race leaders were a bit more lenient with who we dealt with.

Bachman Yard allowed me to start my ministry. It was God's commission for me to start doing His work. I recognized that mission from Ephesians 2:10: *For we are God's handiwork, created in Christ Jesus to do good works, which God prepared in advance for us to do.* I had the freedom in Bachman to hold regular Bible studies, minister across races, and use my commissary to help clothe and feed the less fortunate inmates. James 2:26 inspired me to put truth into action: *As the body without the spirit is dead, so faith without deeds is dead.*

With Bachman Yard also came the privilege of one extra visiting day per week. Saturday was family day for visitation, but Sirarpi came by herself on Sundays, which allowed us to spend the entire day together. Those precious days helped me realize God's blessing on our marriage, and we grew closer despite the bars and chains. We dug into God's Word together, and our bond strengthened in ways I never would have imagined. The truth of God's promise in Jeremiah 33:3 became clear and personal to me: *Call to me and I will answer you and tell you great and unsearchable things you do not know.*

The great and unsearchable things that God showed me were eternal truths. I realized that razor wire, thick doors, and chains could not destroy or break what God had brought together. It was just the opposite. Our trust in God's love and mercy was rewarded with an incredible love and closeness – an unbreakable bond of a cord of three strands (see Ecclesiastes 4:12).

I learned that all I needed to find truth was the Bible (I used the NIV Life Application Study Bible) and the Holy Spirit; it was all there. It was not in emotions, altar calls, or sinner's prayers. It was not in lighting candles, crossing oneself, or worshipping saints. I even learned that there were no altar calls in the Bible. An altar call was a method used to invite those who were seeking God to remain or come forward after the preaching to have their souls dealt with more individually. Some called it the "anxious bench" because those who were anxious or concerned about their souls would come forward to a specific bench appointed for this purpose. Others spoke of an "inquiry room" where those concerned for their souls and were seeking God could go and receive more personal spiritual counsel. This developed into what we now know as an altar call, where the preacher invites people to come forward to the altar. People often made a commitment to God at the altar, and this worked well because people's word was their bond in those days. When they said, "I do," they meant it and followed through. There was nothing wrong with it because the people actually made a commitment and lived accordingly. Because it worked, it has come down through the years.

I discovered that this method is no longer as effective as it used to be. We are a different generation, and our word is not our bond. I attended services in prison where I saw people from different churches come in every week on various days. When they came, the same crowd of inmates attended, answered the altar call, and said a sinner's prayer. Every one of those churches thought they had a group of a dozen men who were saved because of them. That took place four times in one week. I knew something was wrong with this picture, and I realized that the reality of that method creates confusion instead of conversions.

I had been set free spiritually, and now I was about to be set free physically. The clock ticked slowly. It was almost noon. I sat with my Bible on my lap and read Deuteronomy 8. On the yard, I taught that this passage should be required reading for every inmate getting sprung. It contained God's instructions to Joshua and the Israelites before He delivered them from their forty years of wandering in the desert and took them into the Promised Land:

> *Remember how the LORD your God led you all the way in*
> *the wilderness these forty years, to humble and test you in*
> *order to know what was in your heart, whether or not you*

would keep his commands. He humbled you, causing you to hunger and then feeding you with manna, which neither you nor your ancestors had known, to teach you that man does not live on bread alone but on every word that comes out of the mouth of the LORD. (Deuteronomy 8:2-3)

For forty years, God held His people close in the wilderness. During that time, God was faithful. He provided. He revealed His character, His promises, and His unyielding love and mercy. More than that, He was preparing them. The Promised Land was to be a holy place of worship, but it was full of idol worship and horrific sin. God had used the time in the desert to test and humble His people and to raise great warriors such as Joshua in order to engage in the battle ahead to cleanse and prepare the land for His glory.

I looked up at the locked prison door that was soon to open to my freedom. I felt the peace of the Holy Spirit. I sensed Him telling me that my training was complete. I was going to walk out those doors like Joshua crossing the Jordan. In essence, prison was my Bible college. Outside that door was a lost world, a harvest field full of lost souls who desperately needed Christ. God got my attention with a barrier wall, wreckage, and death. He had used a corrupted legal system, incarceration, and loneliness to humble and prepare me. Now the God of eternal love and restoration was sending me.

The clock struck twelve. The doors rolled open. I stood and walked toward freedom, leaving my orange peels in a crumpled heap on the prison floor. As I stepped through the prison gates, I saw Sirarpi walking toward me from the parking lot – free, with her arms open wide. Romans 8:28 burst from my inner being: *And we know that in all things God works for the good of those who love him, who have been called according to his purpose.*

"Here am I, Lord," I said. "The workers are few, and I've seen the plentiful harvest. My training is complete. Here am I, Lord. I'm ready – ready for battle."

Part 5

God Blesses

Chapter 23

New Beginnings

How can a man describe the moment when he steps from incarceration into freedom, from his criminal life to a life with Christ? How can he describe those first steps walking in a free man's shoes and stepping into his wife's arms, free from the confines of cinder block and chains? I brushed Sirarpi's tears of joy from her delicate cheeks and nearly burst with happiness at the thought of returning home to my family after more than twenty months away.

However, I was leaving something behind in that prison, something I would never get back, something I would never experience again: time. Time to spend with God. It struck me hard. With the scent of desert bloom and the first whiff of Sirarpi's sweet perfume, I realized that being in the free man's world meant that I would never again have the opportunity to spend such intimate time with my Lord Jesus Christ.

I had been told that time did not matter in the joint. That was wrong. Time was all I had, and I learned to be diligent with it. I had precious time – time to be alone with God. My time of incarceration was not as much a punishment for my past life as it was a time to become more intimate with Jesus Christ. I knew He would never leave me or forsake me, but as I stepped through those gates, I felt a sense of separation from Him that left a pit in my stomach that still aches to this day.

The ache made me think of Jesus's time on earth. Jesus was broken to the point that His bones were pulled from their joints (Psalm 22:14). He was despised and rejected for His calling, beaten down by the people He loved. He was the Man of Sorrows, *familiar with pain* (Isaiah 53:3). He accepted a calling as an innocent man who was to be pierced and crushed for sins He did not commit (Isaiah 53:5). Jesus persevered over Satan's attacks (see Matthew 4) and accepted God's call. He was refined through trials and pain – from leading His misfit disciples to being nailed to the cross. The refining prepared Him to finish His mission. Then God delivered Him. He is reunited with His Father now, sitting at the right hand of Almighty God and interceding for us. Now God blesses Him as He places all things under His feet and upholds Him as head over everything (Ephesians 1:22). King of kings, His name is above all names (Philippians 2:9; 1 Timothy 6:15).

God was blessing me too. Instead of leaving prison with no clue of how to restart life, I had been allowed by God to begin my new life while in prison. He had given me a vision. In prison, I started leading Bible studies with the men – men who needed Jesus as much as I did, and I could minister across racial and criminal lines.

However, this was also a transition for me. I was now a family man. I had a wife and two children, but my past tugged at me and reminded me of who I had been. I knew that my past could follow me. The cartels were upset with me and threatened me because they saw me as a liability. I knew too much about them and they were not comfortable with me getting out of the business.

Although I had not been aware of it at the time, they had watched me in the packed courtroom. I didn't know who they were, but they would always know what was going on in court. Every day that I sat in court, they were there also, watching and listening. One day as I was leaving, a man approached me. I did not know him, but I soon realized that he was from one of the cartels I had done business with. He told me, "We're here. We're watching – so if you throw a name out there, we will know."

I had conversations with these guys – scary conversations. "I'm out," I'd say. "I don't want to do business anymore."

"You know we can't let you walk away," was their reply.

"I really can, and I'm walking."

"That choice has consequences. Do you understand?"

I replied, "It's a choice I get to make, but you know, life is short, and I get to choose how I die. If I die turning to God, then the legacy I leave behind for my children is that their Papa died young because he turned away from corruption to God's way of life."

The lives of the cartel were on the line, so for them it would have been safer to just take me out to get rid of that problem. But there was enough commitment and experience between us, so they just watched. They had to be cautious. Since I knew certain people who were very deep in the business, I was a particular dangerous risk to them.

Usually, the problem is not just walking away from the business at that level, but the problem is the debt owed. Often when the cartel needs to unload tons of "stuff," they front the supply. If the buyer loses the load or can't get the necessary price, he still owes for it. Soon the cartel owns the buyer. However, because of the structure of my business, because of who I was, and because I was independent, I only took what I could pay for. In the end, I didn't owe them, so I was able to get out. God used that discipline to release me from them, even though I knew their operations and who they were.

I was aware that they might still kill me, but I did this because it was the right thing to do for my family and my new life. The apostle Paul wrote, *I can do all this through him who gives me strength* (Philippians 4:13). I drew the line when it was tough, and I refused to succumb to their threats. I had burned the bridges, so there was no turning back. I was out, and living for Christ was the only option acceptable to me.

But here I am, I didn't die. The Lord protected me once again. It is very tough to make a change, but when we really believe that something is true, we will do whatever it takes to stay the course. Yes, I broke the curse and proved that no matter how messed up we are, all things are possible with Christ. Only Christ could turn my mess into a message of hope. There is hope. There is hope for the moms who are struggling with their kids. There is hope for the kids who are struggling with their addictions. There is hope for all.

I am a new man. I have a new life. I am blessed beyond anything I may have dreamed. Paul also wrote, *If anyone is in Christ, the new creation has come: The old has gone* (2 Corinthians 5:17). Along with the new life came freedom – freedom to work and serve the God who protected me so many times. John 8:32 tells us, *You will know the truth, and the truth will set you free.*

Getting Access

My transition to civilian life was unique in that it began while I was still in prison. I had been able to remain faithful, study God's Word, and share the gospel with anyone who would listen. Also, I had a wife on the outside who faithfully cared for our home and children. We both had looked forward to the day when we could serve our Lord together.

Therefore, when I left prison, we returned to one of the small churches I had connected with previously. However, we soon decided not to continue there. I realized it was time to move on since we didn't feel comfortable with the methods of the Pentecostal religious customs. Besides, Sirarpi had sensed a lack of love and caring there while I was in prison – at a time when she very much needed the support and love of the church family.

We connected with Radiant Church for a time, and that is where Sirarpi decided to be baptized by immersion. Shortly after that, we sold our home in El Mirage, moved to northwest Phoenix, and found Christ's Church of the Valley (CCV), which became our home church. It was only a one-campus church at that time, so we grew with it. I became fully engaged in several weekly Bible study groups, started the nonprofit prison ministry, and continued to run the insurance business. Our church is not perfect, but we chose to love and welcome all sinners without legalism, restrictions, or limitations for newcomers. That helped the church grow very quickly. We had strong leaders with a vision to reach the lost with proactive measures. The freedom not to have to look a certain way, dress a certain way, or talk a certain way led to visitors being comfortable. People were loved, not judged, at CCV. The approach was to love the sinner but to hate the sin that enslaved them. With this vision, the church has been able to open the doors and let God do His work. Eventually, multiple campuses mushroomed all over the valley.

I pursued my vision – the one God gave me while I was on Stiner Red. I understood the words of our Lord to the apostle Paul when He sent him to the gentiles. My heart's desire (Romans 10:1) was to reach the incarcerated population and their loved ones – especially the untouchables, the lepers of today's society. I offered my employees more pay so I could step down from day-to-day operations at the insurance business that I had established before I went to prison. The insurance job was commission based, and I did very well, but because I had been the primary salesman, I sacrificed 40 percent of my income in order to dedicate myself to the ministry. I was willing to make this sacrifice because I was ready to pursue the vision of the ministry that God had set before me. By stepping down, I could focus more on the prison ministry. I could better help other inmates with their spiritual walk and could offer them reentry resources when they are released. There comes a point in a Christian life when perspective must change from an earthly viewpoint to an eternal one. Matthew 6:33 tells us to *seek first his kingdom and his righteousness*. We must choose to transition our perspectives from chasing a selfish life of worldly success to living a life of significance as we make a difference in the lives of others. We must choose to serve our King Jesus, not our selfish desires.

That first ministry, Life Changing Prison Ministry, began in 2005. I had met a man named Del while I was in prison. He would come in and conduct Monday night church services, which I would attend. After I got out, I approached him about helping me start a ministry. He was an accountant, and he knew the legal stuff, so he did all the paperwork and set up the 501(c)(3) for Life Changing Prison Ministry. Chris Hansen was also part of my ministry at that time, and he served on the board. Chris and his wife, Grace, along with Del and I, were the original board members of the first nonprofit prison ministry.

I had been out for a couple of years when a mother somehow got my number and asked me to minister to her son. I told her that I did not have access to the Maricopa County Jail, so I could not visit her son; at least that was my assumption, although I had never checked. However, she was persistent. We had talked on the phone, but I had never met this mother in person. She kept saying, "My son, you know, he wants to talk to you."

I kept telling her, "I don't know how you heard of me, but I can't go in."

Finally one night, I was convicted. I couldn't sleep after I had talked to that mom again. I told myself I would have to do something about it because I didn't want to lose any more sleep. I got up and called the jail.

I said, "Look, here's what I'm asking. Can I come in there for a visit?"

The lady who was doing the coordinating said, "Roger, come in ASAP! Our training is this week, and if you get in right now, I could get you cleared."

I was shocked, this was unexpected. I was able to attend the orientation and apply for a badge. The lady signed me up for the training and told me to wait two weeks for the fingerprinting because I was so close to having been off probation for two years. I did exactly as she said, and I received a badge at Maricopa County Jail, where the son of the woman who kept calling me was housed.

I started visiting him. He was only eighteen. That was my first experience behind the closed doors at 4th Avenue Jail, and it was a scary thing to step back in behind locked doors. But I enjoyed bringing that young man hope. I even looked forward to going back inside Arizona state prisons, but Arizona state had their rules and regulations, and I did not yet qualify. God used this mom to get me in the jail first, and that was obviously God's will and timing. I needed to trust God and His timing for open doors as the ministry moved along.

Going into Juvenile Prison

I also wanted to reach the juveniles. There were two juvenile homes between my home and CCV: Adobe Mountain Boys and Black Canyon Girls Juvenile Corrections. My heart ached as I drove past them every day on my way to mentor inmates in the county jails. I was able to enter on a one-day visitor pass, but was promptly told that my record prohibited me from returning.

I approached Chaplain Soto, who tried to help me, but the director rejected my application because of legal restrictions for ex-felons. Working from the outside, I rallied teams and volunteers who qualified to lead an outreach team in both the boys' and girls' facilities. Within six years, the juvenile ministry grew to more than fifteen volunteers who ministered through church services, mentorships, and events such as soccer clinics, pizza parties, puppet shows, and holiday concerts. The ministry team was able to go in, but without me.

The juvenile ministry worked this way for years, until Governor Brewer appointed a new director who defined the restrictions for ex-felons differently. This opened the doors for a select few ex-felons to be considered for badge access to the juvenile facilities. The bill was signed into law in November of 2012, but with my legal file with the state of Arizona, I did not qualify. However, the staff and leaders of the Arizona Department of Juvenile Corrections were so impressed with my commitment to these kids that they made a way for me to enter the facilities. The new director approved my badge, and on December 1, 2012, I entered Adobe Mountain for the first time in more than six years.

This worked for two years – until a new governor was elected who assigned a different director. This one did not renew my badge. He claimed that the previous director had misinterpreted the legislation. However, my passion and enthusiasm for reaching these young boys and girls made such an impact on the juvenile correctional leadership that for the first time in state correctional history, they asked an ex-felon to join the Directors Religious Council Committee. This allowed me to meet regularly with key decision makers in juvenile corrections, allowing the ministry to have a major impact on how to connect with these kids in life-changing ways. For more than ten years, I have been on their director's leadership committee. I can serve on the committee, but I can't yet go in to visit or talk to the juveniles.

We have had a team of volunteers involved there for the past fifteen years doing the work of God without my presence, and we praise God for that. I will continue to rally the volunteers and delegate leaders. It is not really about me anyway. What is important is that we make a difference in the lives of these kids, and we are doing so, by the grace of God, with our Bibles and the dedication of the multiple volunteers who go in and teach and preach to them every week.

Chapter 24

Ministry Growth

My past disqualified me from visitation rights inside the Arizona Department of Corrections system, so I continued my ministry on a much smaller scale that included one-on-one mentoring, church services, Bible studies, and baptisms at the Maricopa County jails. New mentees only came to me through word of mouth, but my reputation circulated throughout the jails quickly, and the ministry grew.

After a few years, Del and I agreed to disagree on the direction of our mission, and our visions caused us to drift apart. We dissolved the Life Changing Prison Ministry nonprofit organization, and I started a new vessel at my home church called Christ's Church of the Valley Prison Ministry. Just like the apostle Paul and Barnabas parted ways (Acts 15:36-41), so did Del and I, but God continues to use us both, just as God continued to use Paul and Barnabas – to bring hope to others.

After all, Matthew 9:37 says, *The harvest is plentiful but the workers are few.* There is plenty of work for all of us to do. Del stayed focused on his local mission, but I saw the need to expand my vision beyond Phoenix, and eventually worldwide. I have always been extreme in my methods, constantly taking risks – but now I was doing so for good reasons, such as kingdom expansion. I wanted to reach out to incarcerated kids and adults, as well as to their loved ones, but Del was laser-focused on teaching the incarcerated men. Both are great missions, but we inevitably needed to part ways. It was a heartbreaking moment.

It was mandatory for me that I serve Christ for free. I refused to be paid for serving God. That was the only way I felt I could be transparent to everyone about my true motives. It also held me accountable so that I would never be codependent on money for serving God in a way that might derail me from my true mission or put me in a position where I would compromise my convictions for serving our Lord. My past was full of issues driven by greed – money. The reality was that money had been my god and the monster in my life, so I wanted to make sure that money was never going to be a factor in my new life, especially if I was a steward overseeing a ministry. The only way I felt that was possible was to trust God 100 percent, to trust Him with all aspects of my life and ministry, which meant allowing Him to provide everything that was needed to move forward. I would not take pay, and my staff would all be volunteers. All volunteers, including myself, had a self-sustaining income outside of the ministry that allowed the ministry to thrive under the No Staff Paid policy. In my circumstance, the family insurance company covered the bills. Others were retired or had spousal income that provided them with the resources to volunteer with the ministry.

In only a few years, the CCV Prison Ministry grew in such a way that it became its own nonprofit organization known as Rescued Not Arrested, separating it from CCV as an entity, but remaining as a mission partner. We continue to work with the volunteer staff, and the ministry continues to grow and connect with many other like-minded churches. Essentially, we took that partnership model at CCV and became mission partners with many other like-minded churches nationwide.

This arrangement has greatly benefited the ministry in many ways. I have not been derailed by the pressures of finances. I don't get desperate and worried about shutting down due to inability to pay staff or major bills. Initially, I invested a large portion of my own personal funds to make this happen, donating it to the ministry. I self-funded it until it gained enough momentum and partners to thrive on its own. The more donations that came in, the less I needed to fund it myself, and the more the Bible outreach grew.

Church Services, Bible Studies, and Baptisms

Even though I have not been able to go back into the Arizona Department of Juvenile Corrections, I could still go into the Maricopa County jails. Our team conducts one-on-one mentorships, Bible studies, church services, and baptisms at the Maricopa County Sheriff's Office. As the requests for mentorships increased, the need for more mentors grew. I rallied more volunteers so we could meet the demand for more nondenominational services for inmates.

Eventually, we changed the name of the ministry to "Rescued not Arrested" (RNA). We believe that this name truly captures what the ministry is about. It is more than just people ministering at prisons; it is about breaking inmates free of the chains that bind them and showing them that God is a God who saves, not enslaves.

We conducted about forty church services a month in the earlier years of the ministry. As we taught God's Word and shared the gospel, we highlighted the Great Commission as part of the next step each person should take. We don't practice the sinner's prayer or altar calls to invite people to Christ. Instead, we challenge them all to take their time to reevaluate their life purpose and to really understand the truth as they make the most important decision to go all in with Christ for the rest of their lives. A very serious life commitment starts by knowing enough, reading and studying enough, and asking enough.

When individuals are hungry for truth and are convicted to make a commitment, accepting Christ Jesus as their Lord and Savior and understanding and believing that He died for them and rose again on the third day, they can simply make that commitment. As a next step of faith, they can get immersed in water baptism, followed by obedience to God's Word, doing their best and trusting God for the rest. We challenge them to find a Bible-teaching church family and small group Bible study in their community and become involved as soon as they are able to do so. John 15:5 tells us to remain in the vine. Jesus said, *I am the vine; you are the branches. If you remain in me and I in you, you will bear much fruit; apart from me you can do nothing.*

We assure people that we will never be good enough or clean enough to accept Christ, but that we need to come to Him as we are because without the power of the Holy Spirit, we can never change our hearts, minds, and bad habits. Only God through the Holy Spirit can help us overcome the strongholds of this world.

In the past decade, we have baptized many who have chosen to commit themselves to Christ. We stay away from emotional invitations for commitment decisions because they can be too shallow, and although intentions may be good, they are fleeting, and there is usually no follow-up.

While I was in prison, I witnessed many people who wanted to meet the expectations of others and were pressured by them or their emotional feelings from a great sermon to raise their hand and say a sinner's prayer, but then went back to the same lifestyle as before. That leads me to believe that they might not have understood what true commitment to Christ looks like or did not know how to take their next steps. Life service, not lip service, is what matters in the end. That is why we use the approach in Matthew 28:19-20:

> *Therefore go and make disciples of all nations, baptizing them in the name of the Father and of the Son and of the Holy Spirit, and teaching them to obey everything I have commanded you. And surely I am with you always, to the very end of the age.*

Since COVID, RNA has been invited back by federal, state, and county jails to again conduct church services, baptisms, and one-on-one mentorships.

Bibles

After eighteen years, growth continues, and God has provided more than I could have ever imagined, even without us ever doing fundraisers. We've never had financial hardship, and we even thrived during the COVID pandemic when other ministries had to close down. Because of our philosophy of no paid staff and very low overhead, almost all donations went toward Bibles and postage.

The first recipients of the study Bibles were inmates at Lewis Prison, where I had served time. My time In Lewis Prison was like a Bible college for me, and the NIV Life Application Study Bible was the best tool I had to learn God's Word in an understandable language. I knew how valuable that Bible was for me, and I wanted to share it with as many inmates as possible.

One day, I called Zondervan Publishing and asked for a discounted rate on the NIV Life Application Study Bibles. We already had a custom cover on regular NIV Bibles from our initial partnership with Biblica before Zondervan took over their operations; that cover serves as a business card since it has our contact information on it, and eventually we added two of my favorite Bible passages. The back cover has Proverbs 3:5-6: *Trust in the LORD with all your heart and lean not on your own understanding; in all your ways submit to him, and he will make your paths straight.*

Colossians 1:13-14 was later added to the front cover: *For he has rescued us from the dominion of darkness and brought us into the kingdom of the Son he loves, in whom we have redemption, the forgiveness of sins.*

I had first worked to get a regular custom-cover Bible with Biblica Publishing, and then when HarperCollins purchased both Zondervan and Biblica, I asked Gary, my representative, to ask them to consider printing a custom cover for us on their NIV Life Application Study Bibles in both English and Spanish. They eventually agreed, and we have been able to send these Bibles into prisons all over the world.

As far as I know, we are the only partner with Zondervan that has received NIV Life Application Study Bibles with custom covers. In fact, they stopped production and distribution of their Spanish leather study Bible years ago, but they still honor our agreement to this day. Because of this, as of 2023, we have purchased around eight hundred thousand Bibles, including study Bibles, for distribution.

We now have two versions of the custom-cover Bibles in both English and Spanish. One is directed to the incarcerated, and the other is aimed toward the general audience.

When we began this ministry, we only had two volunteers and could only reach dozens of people each month. As of 2023, we have about 150 volunteers and have reached millions of individuals. This is because, through mission partners and chaplains, we have access to thousands of prisons in the United States and 178 countries. In prisons especially, we learned that dozens of people have shared one Bible that we sent, hence rippling our outreach numbers beyond our understanding. God knows how many people have been reached, and that's all that matters. I'm not a big fan of statistics because I know how easily they can be manipulated, but in 2022 alone, RNA paid for and sent out one hundred thousand Bibles. However, we had requests for 1.5 million Bibles, so we continue to pray and ask for God's guidance as we trust Him to provide.

Magazines and Biography

Two years after Rescued Not Arrested (RNA) was formed, *Prison Living Magazine* did an article on my testimony as their cover story. The letters and requests started pouring in. Many inmates had already finished the American Bible Academy study course, which is a requirement to receive a free NIV Life Application Study Bible from us.

In 2014, a biography of my life, *Rescued Not Arrested,* was written by Joe Gammage, an RNA volunteer. We distributed that book along with Bibles to the prisons because my life before and during prison was a story that many prisoners, if not most, could relate to. It has touched the hearts of thousands of inmates and has led them to pursue their own relationship with God.

For example, Robbie recently wrote:

I am the only person in my entire family who has received Jesus Christ as Savior. I grew up in the streets of South Phoenix. I've been raised around drugs and violence my entire life. I was "jumped" into a gang at the age of seven and was a troublemaker until three years ago.

Your saying, "Rescued not Arrested," is by all counts the truth for me. I am sitting here fighting many cases – first-degree murder being one – and I can honestly say now that I have the love of Jesus Christ. I am ready for whatever the outcome of my incarceration is. I have given it all over to the Lord and have chosen to let His will be done.

Now I am a "Bible Thumper" – the same thing I used to laugh at people for being. I get proud when people discover I'm a Christian. I'm not ashamed. I have you and your ministry to thank for that. So, from the bottom of my heart, thank you for helping to save me.

In 2020, *Victorious Living Magazine,* a nationally distributed magazine that delivers hope behind bars and introduces incarcerated people to Jesus Christ and the God of second chances, published my testimony as their cover story on their February 2020 issue. In March, following the COVID outbreak, that issue was distributed, and inmates read about my family's immigration process and how we came to Los Angeles with few possessions and many dreams, but experienced disrespect and poverty. I told about how I was overwhelmed trying to fit into the US culture and the mixed racial society at the age of nine in the Los Angeles projects with major language barriers. I desperately hungered to belong with the kids in my community and looked for acceptance and love in all the wrong places. I quickly learned to steal and deal drugs to make money to get the attention I was seeking. It worked for a while, until the consequences started catching up with me. I talked about becoming an ambitious businessman who networked with cartel leaders in the drug industry and distributed tons of marijuana across the nation. Many prisoners were able to identify with my background and my time in prison.

What was shocking to most of them was how I got out of that lifestyle. God had continually reminded me that He was there – waiting for me to trust Him. Now I get to serve Him. I get to be the hands and feet of Jesus as He rescues others with my message of hope. Yes, we can truly do all things through Christ, who gives us strength (Philippians 4:13).

We know that many people around us feel isolated and alone, whether in prison or in a free society. They think that their actions have disqualified them from the love of Christ. Some people have never been introduced to Him, even while sitting in their own churches, but all people need to turn to the Lord in faith and obedience, and trust Him for their salvation.

Another article was published in 2021 about the Rescued Not Arrested Ministry. Chris Moon of the *Christian Standard* wrote an article titled "Arizona Prison Ministry Making Global Impact." Chris emphasized that this ministry distributes tens of thousands of Bibles every year to jails and prisons across the United States and to mission fields around the globe. This has been possible through partnerships with other organizations. David's Well Ministry in Panama has received thousands of Spanish NIV Bibles, NIV Life Application Study Bibles, and RNA books of my testimony. Their mission is to take the gospel to native villages in Panama and other Central American countries. Spanish materials are not abundant in these countries, so these materials are particularly cherished.

When Christian Resources International partnered with us, a new door opened, giving us access to 178 countries. A connection was made with trusted leaders in multiple countries, and we were able to send containers full of Bibles and books to thousands of people overseas.

RNA has sent more than fifty thousand Bibles since COVID to orphanages, leper colonies, and other places in dozens of countries. We had already done some work internationally, but this partnership extended our outreach immensely.

COVID and Correspondence

God's outreach, Rescued Not Arrested, also offers correspondence outreach to all inmates nationwide. We call it our mail mentorship program. It is like a spiritual pen-pal program to thousands who are incarcerated all across the country. Our letter-writing outreach is growing by the minute, bringing hope from our living rooms to hopeless people in prisons nationwide. In like manner, the Bible is a letter of instructions from God to us! B-I-B-L-E = **B**asic Instructions **B**efore Leaving Earth.

The magazine articles, biography, and partnerships put us in a position to serve inmates when others had to shut down due to the COVID pandemic. In-person programs were shut down in prisons, but thousands of the RNA Bibles were already in prison pods and jail cells, and all of them had our contact information on the cover. Faced with loneliness and more isolation, inmates wrote to us. In fact, they flooded our "spiritual pen-pal" program with letters. One coordinator wrote, "Now more than ever, our inmates need these resources in an environment of extended isolation during the COVID-19 crisis."

A chaplain wrote, "Most are reconnecting with God as they struggle with their current lifestyle, and we have found that some are connecting with God for the first time. . . . Plus, the inmates often ask for books on real-life stories to encourage them that being here does not define who they are."

My biography has often ignited the spark that they needed to pursue God for themselves through the Bible. I encourage them to not allow their past to ever again determine their identity, but I tell them that their identity should be in Christ only. We can find true hope and freedom in Him. During the pandemic, everything except the mail had stopped. All that the inmates had was time, so requests for more Bibles and mail mentors increased overnight. I believe that God is using my story as a bridge to His story, and it is working like a charm.

A Texas chaplain tells us that the resources we send are much appreciated and are a great source of spiritual guidance, especially during this time of reflection for the inmates. Another chaplain told us about a lady from South America who had received one of our Bibles. "She was so grateful that her Spanish Bible had arrived that she jumped up and down with excitement. She had tears in her eyes and told me 'Thank you' three times."

But it's not just the chaplains who write to thank us. Letters come from all over the country from inmates who tell their stories, and they are a powerful witness to the value of our ministry. Typically, inmates are given the opportunity to complete the American Bible Academy Bible study correspondence course. Upon completion of that course, they are automatically gifted a Rescued Not Arrested NIV Life Application Study Bible. An ex-inmate explained how much the ABA course and the RNA Study Bible helped him. Kevin said:

For almost three years, I served my incarceration.... I was introduced to ABA and Set Free Ministries. My love for the Lord grew stronger, and I have put all my hope, desires, and needs in His hands.... The ABA studies helped me comprehend God's plans for us all, as well as understand who He is and how He loves us all. With my new life that I have been given, I see things clearer through God's eyes and not the world's.

Another student/inmate finished the ABA course and was surprised when the NIV Life Application Study Bible arrived for him. He said, "This is a very precious gift.... I can think of no better way to spend my time than to spend it studying God's Word."

Likewise, Derrick wrote, "God continues to bless me daily, even in here. Praise the Lord! I received your Bible and have not put it down. The study guide has helped me to better understand the passages, as it puts them in words that I can understand and comprehend."

Another inmate hit the nail on the head when he said, "This new Bible is more than just a gift in the mail. It is my lifeline to God Himself." That is what it is for all of us, but sometimes we need to be confined before we discover that truth.

Many letters come simply as a thanksgiving for the Bibles, books, visits, and services. One particular letter said that my message of hope, redemption, and trusting in Jesus was perfect for them. God's Word of salvation is always perfect, and He blesses me to be the messenger time after time. A chaplain in Maryland said, "The inmates love to read testimony books about lives that have been redeemed. It gives them hope for their future. God is faithful, and He is still in the business of saving lost souls and putting them on the right path."

My desire is to bring hope – to show the way from doubt and disbelief to trusting only Jesus Christ, our Lord and Savior. That was my experience, and I believe He desires all people to trust Him. A chaplain in Georgia indicated that the Bibles "fly off the shelves." He said they have more men and women coming to Sunday services and more inmates participating in devotions and Bible study than ever before. God wants to free us from empty traditions, addictions, corruption, and selfish ways. Prison has a way of offering people limited temptation and a chance to say no to their addictions or bad choices and setting them on a path to life – a life of freedom. Even though drugs and hooch are far too often available in prisons, that environment really limits access to them, and they become more difficult to afford. In addition, the consequences can be fatal if one falls into debt because of drugs or gambling.

Another chaplain in Georgia observed that "the Word of God is one of God's greatest blessings given to us. To have God's holy spoken word in written form is the most powerful example of love that we can give those incarcerated in our prisons. I find it so amazing how the Word of God is the one thing that just about every inmate asks for when they arrive at my facility. . . . It gives them hope." Truly, *the Word of God is alive and active. Sharper than any double-edged sword, it penetrates even to dividing soul and spirit, joints and mar-row; it judges the thoughts and attitudes of the heart* (Hebrews 4:12).

Those who are arrested have two specific needs: they need a human story of redemption, and they need to be able to know and understand God's Word. My personal story of transformation and healing assures people that by living for Jesus, they, too, can find a path to a new way of life, hope, and truth. Second, our NIV Bibles and study Bibles in both English and Spanish offer them a simple way to read and understand the Bible, especially if they are reading the Scriptures for the first time.

Some individuals have had life stories similar to mine. Christian wrote:

I came across your book *Rescued Not Arrested*, and it completely changed my life. I can relate to so much of it. . . . I fell in love with making money. My brother and I were arrested for possession of a controlled substance with intent to deliver. We were convicted in trial and sentenced to forty years in the Arkansas Dept. of Corrections. We found God while in prison, and even got baptized. . . . One year into my sentence, I saw my name on the local news, and it said that my appeal went through. In a few weeks, I was released with no record; it was reversed and dismissed. God gave me a second chance at life, but I began a downward spiral and started using drugs. I ended up back in jail. I felt so ashamed that God saved my life and got me out of a forty-year sentence, yet I ended up back in the jail system.

But I read your book and felt something inside me come back on. I started praying and requested a Bible. I got the Rescued Not Arrested Bible, which came as a sign to me that God has a plan and that all of this will be used for His greater good. I now know that I want to serve God and mentor young inmates and veterans. God has been so good to me, and no matter what I've done, Jesus loves me and never leaves me. I feel no anxiety about my sentencing because the will of God will be done. Thank you so much.

We get hundreds of letters each month from across the country, and a team of volunteers writes personal responses to each of them. Some simply want to know who Christ is and how they can change their lives. Others want to tell their own stories. Many come to realize that their arrest is really part of their rescue from something – an addiction, a toxic relationship, or even a tradition. Their arrest can be a time for God to work in their lives. Their own words prove how great of an effect the Word of God has had on their lives.

As prison facilities opened back up after COVID, we revamped our in-person church services in the Arizona prisons. Pre-COVID, we held hundreds of services a month, and now I even do video conferencing with inmates as part of our mentoring program.

Reentry Assistance

The latest exciting and effective outreach for RNA is our reentry programs. Although our network of support and resources are mostly in Arizona for now, I pray that this model will eventually expand to other states.

In 2017, RNA was approached by two separate departments of the Arizona Department of Corrections (AZDOC). First, we developed a twelve-month, faith-based reentry mentorship program to be used with the men and women incarcerated in prisons across the state. It was a long process and a lot of work, but the curriculum was completed in April 2018, presented to AZDOC, and approved for use. We started piloting that program at Tucson prisons with the partnership of volunteers from a local Tucson Christian church.

This curriculum gave us an opportunity to supply mentors who would spend time with incarcerated men and women and provide them with resources that would help inmates grow spiritually and develop a reentry plan. The best part is that these mentors can continue to work with these people after they are released to help them walk out their faith and succeed in their transition from prison. Those who follow our advice are most likely to succeed. Our local ministry has helped hundreds gain employment, housing, and church group support when they are released from prisons.

The curriculum covers topics such as budgeting, transportation, housing, relationships, and healthy behavior, along with many other skills needed by a man or woman coming home from incarceration. Our role is to assess the inmates' situations and provide them with jobs, housing, and church family opportunities a few weeks before they are released. Our opportunities to use this program continue to increase, as do the opportunities to share this program with churches and organizations that are willing to help those who need a solid orientation back into society.

The encouragement, opportunities, and resources for those who are released are paramount in their success outside of prison. Help with that reentry is most important in order to avoid returning to prison. Our jails and prisons seem to have revolving doors, which we hope to change with our program and God's power to change hearts.

Interestingly, many inmates know they need help fitting back into society, but don't know where to find that help. One inmate recently wrote:

I self-surrendered for new charges, but I am ultimately seeking help with reentering back into society. I have been in and out of jail since 2019, because every time I am released, I don't know where to go, and I end up returning back to the hood and relapsing. I want to stop disappointing my kids and family. I am hoping that if you're not able to help me directly, maybe you can provide me with good resources for reentry.

Daniel was another individual who needed our help. He had moved to Arizona, but a toxic relationship and alcoholism landed him in 4th Avenue Jail, lonely and suicidal. He planned to end it all until someone invited him to an RNA jail church service on a Wednesday night. He told me that Levi, our preacher for that service, spoke directly to him and put him in tears. Soon after that, he requested visits from RNA, and John and Tom visited him weekly

– teaching God's Word and encouraging him to contact us when he got out so we could provide a job, a church family, and housing opportunities. While incarcerated, he requested to be baptized. I saw his paperwork come through, but before we could schedule his baptism, he was released.

After a few weeks, he called and asked for assistance because he had no family in Arizona. Our RNA leaders in East Valley picked him up to attend CCV Mesa. He now is in the CCV small group and has a job opportunity that he is pursuing. Levi and I then had the privilege to baptize him at CCV Peoria. His testimony of a changed life is similar to those we see every month.

Our churches and humanitarian organizations need to understand the desire that these individuals have in regard to being successful outside of prison. When they want to be fruitful servants of God and live productive lives, they need God's love poured out upon them.

The second request I received from the Arizona Department of Corrections regarding reentry was from the Second Chance Program. They invited RNA to conduct weekly events to all selected inmates at the Perryville, Tucson, and Lewis prisons, initially starting at Sunrise Unit, and then Eagle Point, and eventually, years later, transferring to Phoenix West. This was a unique opportunity to share my story and speak truth and life to all audiences from different backgrounds and religious beliefs. Some were even agnostic or atheist. My simple message to all of them was that I am doing this for free because I care enough to help them with jobs, housing, and support-system opportunities when they are released, regardless of their past or religious preferences. I never shy away from telling everyone that I am a Christian, but I promise them I will never push my convictions on them. I agree to disagree on religious and political issues, but I continue to respect and love them for who they are and will offer them my genuine support, regardless of our differences.

Chapter 25

Where Are They Now?

As the ministry has grown, the current path of my life has crossed the paths of many individuals from my other life. Simen pushed his case to trial, and he beat the rap. As the state of Arizona was assembling the jury for his trial, he visited a plastic surgeon and had his face altered just enough so that the witnesses could not make a positive identification on him. He walked – a free man. Although his surgeon was able to change his features enough to set him free from prison, the gifted doctor could not change his heart. Simen eventually went down on a federal drug charge several years later.

Sally D's choices landed him homeless and in the streets, where he dealt drugs for survival. I didn't recognize him the day I responded to his cry for help from his jail cell. I went to visit him at the 4th Avenue Jail. Halfway through my visit with him, I saw a flicker of recognition in his sorrowful, pleading eyes.

"I know you, don't I?" I said.

"Yeah. It's me, man. Sally D. I was your DJ once. You put a gun to my head."

"Now I want to put a Bible in your hand."

"Man, I was *it* back then, wasn't I? What happened to me?"

He had built a file so thick that he finally got sent up on a ten-year stretch for his final charge – a petty theft of a bong pipe from a downtown smoke shop.

Rizzo cleaned up his act, but he hasn't yet discovered the peace that comes from Christ's ability to completely erase his past. Not long ago on a family ski trip, I saw him ahead of me in the lift line. As a joke, I walked up behind him, stuck my finger in his back, and said, "This is it, Rizzo."

His face flushed white, and he looked like he might drop dead. He didn't understand what I meant when I called him brother and told him all was forgiven. Yeah, he's leading a clean life, but he continues to look back, fearing the day when someone comes up behind him with a real gun.

Despite my efforts with Nufo, he continued through the revolving doors of prison gates, getting sent up regularly on everything from domestic disputes with his latest shack-up to beefs involving burglary. He had fallen off the radar for a time, but then I learned where he was and worked with him to change his life.

I had met Nufo the night he tried to hijack my truck. Instead of killing him as would have been standard protocol, I made a business deal with him. He became my "runner," transporting drugs from Phoenix to Michigan. We worked the criminal scene together for a number of years, but after my Damascus Road experience, I was no longer the same person. I had changed. I had broken the cycle, but Nufo still struggled as he worked the business. I tried to win him over, and I consoled him when he went to prison. My team of volunteers and I continued to mentor Nufo. We gave him a Bible, but he was in and out of the system. We were on a journey with him, even though he had not experienced the transformation of life in Christ.

The last time he got out, I sent him to one of our partner ministries that helps with transitioning. This discipleship program is a sober-living environment and is free to those who need it. Nufo participated in the twelve-month in-house program with good Bible study courses. He was even baptized there.

However, Nufo had a weakness – females. Toxic relationships with females often keep these men going through the revolving doors of prison. They do their time and have good intentions coming out, but before long their wives or girlfriends get them to cross over and get back to that life – again and again and again. Ninety-nine percent of the men I minister to can relate to these toxic relationships that drag them down.

Because of this, I emphasize the truth of 1 Corinthians 15:33 to all inmates: *Do not be misled: "Bad company corrupts good character."* It is paramount that bad influences of the past are left behind, and that new, godly relationships are pursued that will build up instead of tear down.

In the end, Nufo lost his battle. He was in a county jail when COVID hit. The lockdown was more than he could handle because he could no longer meet with a mentor – or anyone else. He tied bedsheets together and tried to hang himself by throwing himself from a second-floor balcony. He was rushed to the hospital and put on a ventilator. I went to the hospital as the family had to make the decision to pull the plug because he was declared brain-dead, and I prayed with them and was able to give comfort to the brothers, sisters, nephews, and the rest of the family.

They asked me to do the funeral, even though it had been a long time since I had seen them. They had never met the new me. I was not the same Roger they had known, but they had always respected me and what I did for Nufo. He had made a lot of bad choices before I met him, but I had been able to put some discipline in him when his life was out of control with no structure. They seemed to think I was good for him despite the dark world we worked in because I took him under my wing and gave him a little bit of structure.

Doing the funeral gave me the opportunity to minister to them all together as well as individually. I shared the gospel with them, prayed with them, and gave them hope, which they desperately needed during this dismal time. I invited them to church and small groups. I reached out to the whole family, consoling and comforting them. Nufo's sister did not even recognize this new Roger, and neither did his mother, whose name means "hope," and hope is what I wanted to bring them. There is always hope.

Chapter 26

Testimonies of Real People with Genuine Life Changes

Author of the Original *Rescued Not Arrested*

We all have purpose in our God-given talents, and I already knew in the third grade that I wanted to be a writer – a *New York Times* best-selling mystery/suspense writer.

Writing success became an obsession to me, but after accumulating enough rejection slips, I stopped submitting my work. Fear of success put me in a writing slump, so I chased a business career and started a family, knowing I was letting fear rob me of God's purpose for His gifts.

Then I met Roger Munchian – a twelve-time convicted felon who had done more in his life than my creative mind could ever conjure. I started writing Roger's story, *Rescued Not Arrested*, and thought I had God all figured out. But that was in 2008, and we were losing everything when the global financial meltdown bled my business dry.

Rescued Not Arrested was to be the *New York Times'* best seller that would launch my literary success and restore my finances. I was chasing my talents, but forgot the One who had given them to me. The financial meltdown continued, and we lost more – our houses, our savings, and eventually our marriage.

Everything collapsed, including the book. Now I was a single father of two, and I found myself one day sobbing on the bathroom floor in pitch darkness because I did not want to look at that man in the mirror. I wanted to end it all. However, Roger called. He reminded me of my worth to God and His love for me. He helped me see Christ's rescue mission for me, and I heard Jesus say, "Get up, Joseph, and trust Me."

Feeling peace for the first time, I got up. Later that day I went over to Roger's house, and we sat by the fire pit. He talked me through a lot of stuff. He convinced me not to worry about the book, which took a load off my mind and allowed me to focus on healing. That gave me time to step back and let God heal me. Later, believing it would give me purpose, Roger encouraged me to finish the book.

I wish I could say that the writing passion returned to me, but it didn't. It was my new search for purpose that drove me back to the keyboard. I finished the book, which has impacted lives for nearly ten years, but in 2023 Roger felt that it was time for an updated edition to the book – and this time I wouldn't be writing it. I felt a loss. The final sentence had been written in my literary life, ending with a solid period where I wished I could have put a comma.

But when you seek God's significance over your success, He reminds you of His purpose. The top drawer of my file cabinet is jammed with my ministry folder that is bulging with letters received from incarcerated men and women who shared the impact that Roger's story had on their lives. It's not the type of fan mail that an author receives along with six-figure royalty checks, but it is far richer. For lack of space, let me share just two of these stories.

In the summer of 2020, I received a letter from Cynthia, who was in the Texas correctional system. COVID quarantine meant 24/7 lockdown in a toxic cell pod, being confined to bunks that were less than three feet apart. Cynthia had decided to end her life, but a copy of Roger's story appeared on a book cart that rolled past her bunk. She took the book and read it. Then she wrote, "Your story gives me hope; for this, I need to keep breathing."

A life saved – that is a royalty check with figures that run off the parchment!

The other letter was from Arnulfo (Nufo). He was one of the few "characters" I had met while writing the book. His arrest reconnected him with Roger. He was inspired by the prospect of a book and seeing the new Roger, but when he was released, he fell off our radar.

By the time Arnulfo's path crossed RNA again, *Rescued Not Arrested* had been published, and although we could not mentor him, the book could. After reading the book, he renewed his commitment to Christ. After getting baptized, he wrote to us, "I'm a new creation and am ready to do whatever it is that the Lord wants."

Although his heart was solid for Christ, his struggles ended when he took his own life in his final visit to the county jail. I watched Roger choke back his grief as he gave Arnulfo's eulogy.

However, the purpose of RNA is to tell the story of the hope of Christ's rescue, no matter the depth of depravity or despair, and to save souls for eternity. Although Roger's heart was broken at the loss of his friend, the eulogy became an opportunity for him to share Arnulfo's faith journey with grieving loved ones who were also in need of Christ's rescue.

Success is fleeting. I may not be on the *New York Times* Best Sellers list, but I now focus on using the gifts God gave me for His purpose. There were countless moments when I served in the RNA prison ministry that gave me purpose and saved my life. I now serve with a renewed sense of passion and confidence rather than fear because the purpose of Christ's rescue is eternal. Only God's purpose can put a comma where we put a period.

—H. Joseph Gammage, Author of *Rescued Not Arrested* (2014)

Attracted to the Handcuff Bible

I was in jail when I surrendered my life to Jesus Christ in 2015. Almost immediately, I desired to read God's Word. As soon as I hit the yard at Perryville Women's Prison, I met other Christian women and started to attend church services and Bible study. One day, a friend of mine was carrying a beautiful big Bible with an illustration of broken handcuffs and the words "Rescued Not Arrested" on the cover. I was drawn to this Bible, so I inquired how I could get one. She gave me the address, and I went straight to my cell and wrote a letter to the Rescued Not Arrested Ministry and requested a Bible.

Within two weeks, I was holding my very own NIV Life Application Study Bible in my hands. It was a life-changing gift, and for the next two-and-a-half years, I spent every day in the Word of God, learning everything I could. The RNA Bible was one of my primary tools for building my faith and strengthening my relationship with the Lord.

Soon after my release in 2017, I contacted Roger Munchian, the founder of RNA. I shared my testimony with him and thanked him for the Bible that had helped me so much. Then I traveled to meet Roger and pick up some Bibles for my roommates back at the halfway house. I didn't know it then, but the Lord was positioning me to answer the call He had on my life.

"You have an amazing testimony, Christina," Roger told me during our first meeting. "It was very well written. Do you like to write?"

I told him that I had always wanted to be a writer, but my life had just gotten off track. Roger encouraged me not to underestimate what God might still do in and through my life.

Roger soon invited me to serve as part of the correspondence ministry team at RNA. From then on, I opened all the mail, processed Bible requests, and responded to letters from inmates all over the country. I used writing to encourage others and point them to God's Word as a source of comfort during their dark times. That was almost five years ago, and today I still have the privilege of serving with the RNA team wherever I am needed.

Thank you, Roger and everyone at RNA, for the amazing kingdom work you tirelessly do. The passion and dedication of the people in this ministry have helped the Word of God reach inmates throughout the United States and internationally. Every time a Bible makes its way into the hands and hearts of our incarcerated brothers and sisters, lives will be radically transformed by Jesus, just like mine was.

—Christina (O'Brien) Kimbrel

Prison Yard Is Now His Mission Field

For the first time in my life, in January of 2011, I was arrested and put in jail. I lost everything I had ever worked for. My aviation career of more than thirty years went down the drain. My marital relationship was strained because of the hurt I had caused my wife. In a free fall, it doesn't take long to hit rock bottom.

Little did I know that I would soon be rescued. Like many others, I thought I was beyond saving. I had many opportunities in the past to change my life, but I didn't take advantage of them. In county jail, a few denominational services were offered, as well as one that Roger offered. Whenever possible, I would attend this inspiring Spirit-filled service, but they limited how many could attend. When they didn't open my cell door, I was disappointed because I really looked forward to it. Emphasis was placed on seeking the truth, developing and building a relationship with Jesus, and reading Scripture in context. They emphasized where salvation comes from and all that Jesus did for us – the gospel of God's grace.

I continued my personal Bible studies and saw Roger at the services. I later met with him through his one-on-one mentorship, and I shared with others what Roger shared with me. With his help, my root grew, and I continued my Bible studies. I also enrolled in the correspondence Bible study course that he recommended.

I had to fight the negative and depressing surroundings in jail and lean on the Word of God for my strength. The devil is always ready to uproot us if we allow him to.

My greatest trial was on February 16, 2013. I woke early that morning, feeling as if something terrible had happened. I reached for my Bible in order to read some verses to give me comfort. As I flipped the pages to get to where I had been reading, it fell open to the heading "Ezekiel's Wife Dies" (Ezekiel 24:15-18). My heart sank. I tried to call my wife – many times – unsuccessfully. Then I called my brother who lived near her. I had a bad feeling. Much later that afternoon, after not hearing anything, I was informed that I had a video visit. This was unexpected. On the video, my brother told me that my wife of more than thirty-four years had passed away. Through my tears, I prayed with questions of why, but I immediately thanked the Lord for the years that we had together. I was not going to allow the devil to bring guilt into the picture.

The jail chaplain was either too busy or just didn't want to be bothered to see me. What I didn't know was that my brother had remembered me mentioning Roger's name. He didn't know his last name, but quickly found him on his prison ministry website. He had already called Roger and explained what had happened. Roger made a special trip down to the jail that weekend to see how I was doing and to strengthen me with Scripture. He did not do this out of obligation, but from the heart. This meant so much to me that he was there to help me through such a terrible time. I often think of 2 Corinthians 1:3-4 and of the comfort and compassion that Roger gave me in my time of need.

Roger and his ministry make a difference in many people's lives. He puts a Bible in everyone's hands who asks. It is like Jesus said in Matthew 7:7: *Ask and it will be given to you; seek and you will find; knock and the door will be opened to you.* Roger operates on this scriptural principle. He has inspired me to develop and lead different Bible studies and to help others grow in their walk with Christ.

After three years in county jail, I was sentenced to fifteen years in prison. I write this from behind the prison walls. The state has chosen to punish me with a total of fifteen years of incarceration for my crimes, but Christ has chosen to forgive me, to completely forget my past, and to bless me with an eternity of freedom from the chains of man – and of my own making.

After the news of my wife's passing, I knew I had lost everything on the outside. There is nothing out there for me. The prison is now my mission field where I share the good news. Despite the thick walls and razor wire, I am truly free in Christ, and I get to show other prisoners how they can find that freedom for themselves. I can't think of a more important mission. Christ has chosen to use my brokenness to set the lost and hopeless free.

Roger shared with me how important our testimony is by referencing Revelation 12:11: *They triumphed over him by the blood of the Lamb and by the word of their testimony; they did not love their lives so much as to shrink from death.* I continue to stay in touch with Roger and Rescued Not Arrested, and I include them in my prayers. In January 2026, God willing, I will be released from prison.

Roger, thank you for doing God's will and helping us all to be rescued through Jesus our Lord. The Lord is truly number one in my life, and I pray that you will allow the team at Rescued Not Arrested to help guide you in the truth. I thank the Lord for sending you and your ministry into my life. You will certainly say on that day the words of 2 Timothy 4:7: *I have fought the good fight, I have finished the race, I have kept the faith.* May God bless you in abundance through the knowledge of God and of Jesus our Lord.

—Dan Wharton, Christ's missionary to the lost behind bars

Mother of Young Offender Finds Hope as Her Son Finds Christ behind Bars

During the most frightening and overwhelming times after my son's arrest, Roger Munchian visited him in county jail. I had found Roger's name and number listed on our church website under "Prison Ministry."

Because I didn't know who to turn to or who to trust, this godly man was most reassuring to me. Roger introduced my son, Matt, to the gospel and gave him hope for a future no matter what happened to him. He had an easygoing way of making my son feel valued and accepted while slowly presenting the truth and comfort of God's Word to him.

As my son grew more interested in the Bible, Roger spent time one-on-one mentoring him and helping him gain an eternal perspective on his life. My son began attending church services in the jail, and word quickly spread of this minister who accepted them unconditionally and did not seem to care about the charges they were facing. All were equal in his eyes, and they learned that Jesus sees them all as sinners needing a Savior.

Small Bible studies sprouted up among the guys, and my son took the initiative to lead one. As the seeds were planted, I saw a change in him, and he began to accept his situation and the consequences he faced. This stressful situation was turned into an opportunity for tremendous growth and maturing in his walk with the Lord. My son accepted Jesus as his personal Savior.

Roger continued to keep in touch with him throughout his sentence. Another volunteer from RNA wrote to him during this time. Roger has been an invaluable help to me also. He is there whenever I need to call on him for any type of help or encouragement. I well up with tears when I hear of the amazing things that are evolving through the Rescued Not Arrested Ministry. Not only are offenders being rescued from a life of darkness, but some are returning to the jails after release to minister and help with baptisms.

Roger's dedication and commitment has allowed RNA to grow

from a tiny one-man outreach into a very powerful influence in our jails and prisons. He has been obedient to God's call on his life and inspires so many to follow and serve and trust God for the results.

As an update about my son, Roger and RNA have been an underlying anchor. Their support throughout Matt's time in county jail, prison, and during reentry has meant so much to Matt and our family. They helped Matt secure a job and gave him the confidence that life can still be meaningful, even with the restrictions of probation. Roger has instilled in Matt the truth that God has a plan for his life. He holds a job in a part of the city where he sees so much human hopelessness and suffering, yet Matt has allowed God to soften his heart, and he has jumped in to serve the least of these many times. Through consistent prayers and trust in God's perfect timing, doors have been opened to finally reunite him with his son whom he had lost contact with thirteen years ago. I am very thankful for all the blessings, but especially for the ministry of Roger and RNA.

—Nancy Morrow

Rescued from Trauma to Peace in Prison

After losing my son in a car accident, two of his friends in a motorcycle accident, and then his girlfriend in a deliberate incident, I thought my heart had been wrenched from within me. I blamed God for all my pain and heartache. I was so overwhelmed that I couldn't breathe. I started drinking and using Xanax to numb that pain, but that only led to stronger drugs and more bad decisions. When I was arrested, I was an emotional mess and wanted to die.

While in jail, I started reading the Bible, and then I got the book *Rescued Not Arrested*. These books gave me hope. I lay in bed and cried to God to help me. I told Him I was broken and hurt and didn't know what to do. I repented and asked God for forgiveness.

I accepted Jesus as my Savior on January 4, 2019, and experienced unbelievable peace. The pain and anxiety were gone. I contacted the RNA ministry and requested a visit. It was a blessing when I heard my name called for a visit a few days later. I met a very kind and sweet lady from RNA named Pat. She prayed with me, and we studied the Bible. She was a gift from God. I am so thankful for those who minister through RNA.

After my sentencing, I felt free, even though I was going to prison. I was excited to spend this time getting to know Jesus and His perfect plan and will for my new life. I contacted Roger and asked for a study Bible, and he sent it to me along with other study materials. That Bible was and is my most precious possession. I spent several hours every day reading it. My faith grew, and I became stronger in Christ. I stayed in contact with Roger. He was so kind to always write back to me.

Upon my release, I contacted Roger and let him know that I was out. He set me up with a job, and I started work that same week. He gave me the address of the closest CCV church, and I started attending. I called him a few weeks later and let him know how I was doing, and I talked to him about getting baptized. We set the date, and I was baptized on September 13, 2020.

I got a new job a few months later, and I called Roger to let him know that they hire felons here and that he could give my number to anyone who needs a job. He has sent more than a hundred men and women to me, and they have been hired and given a second chance. God is now using me in mighty ways.

God bless you, Brother Roger and RNA, for all you do in reaching the incarcerated. I am forever grateful for what you have done for me – for being that light in my darkest moments when I was incarcerated. You gave me hope. You discipled me. You are a powerful child of God. Because of your obedience to God, I am walking in the promised land today. I am free; whosoever the Son sets free is free indeed (John 8:36).

God has broken every chain off me. He has taken my broken and shattered life and has made me whole and complete. He has overflowed me with His hope, love, peace, and joy. I am a child of God and am truly grateful for you, Roger, and for your ministry. Now I am blessed to have a part in RNA.

God has once again blessed me with a new job. I am now working with women in their recovery, and I get to share Jesus with them and love them back to life the way Jesus has loved me. I am eternally grateful to the RNA ministry for all they've done for me and continue to do for others. I can only praise God for such obedient servants.

—Jennifer Clark

Diagnosed with Life-Threatening Disease behind Bars, Inmate Finds Eternal Life

I started going to services with Roger while at Maricopa County's 4th Avenue Jail. This was my first time ever in jail, so it was quite stressful for me and my family. I went to the service because I had heard that Roger was from Christ's Church of the Valley (CCV), the church I attended on the outside. It was so easy to relate to his style of teaching because he had been in my shoes; he knew what I was going through. Although I had attended church, I was not saved and had not accepted Christ as my Savior. That happened because of Roger's spiritual mentoring.

A few months after accepting Jesus Christ as my personal Savior, I was diagnosed with Hairy Cell Leukemia. They put me in complete isolation in the jail infirmary. They stripped me of all my personal possessions and locked me away in a glassed-in infirmary cell. Roger came to see me and tried to get a Bible to me, but they would not let him give me a Bible. He argued with them and would not give up. He knew that I needed to have the Word of God in that isolation cell. Eventually they told him that the only way they could allow a Bible in my cell was if it was brand-new and wrapped. Roger left and returned promptly with a brand-new, wrapped Bible that he was able to get into my hands. I could only imagine the looks on their faces when Roger walked back in holding that new Bible.

Roger prayed with me, and I was totally at peace with whether I lived or died because I knew I was going to be with Jesus, and I gave it all to Him. And for that, I will always be in debt to Roger for getting me to that point in my life through his ministry.

Eight years and seven months later, I was released from prison, and Roger was right there for me when I got out. He arranged for me to attend services at CCV and join a men's group, but my first probation team refused to let me do either of those. Eight months later, I had my probation revoked, and I was sentenced to another ten years for my first violation.

Again, Roger was right there. His book and my study Bible were there with me in prison almost as soon as I arrived. During my appeal, I discovered why his work distributing Bibles all over the world was so important. During COVID, I was stuck in isolation for nearly thirty days. The only thing allowed was Roger's book and the Bibles he distributes to the prisons. I don't have the words to describe how thankful I was to have those two items to read in a 24/7 lockdown, when I was only able to go outside for an hour and shower, which only happened five times during those thirty days.

By the grace of God, I won my appeal, which I am told only happens less than 1 percent of the time. I was released for the second time – five years and two months early. And there was Roger again. He set me up to attend CCV and go to the men's group. We scheduled my baptism for October 19, 2022. I had waited more than twelve years for this because I wanted to be baptized at CCV, my home church. My sister custom-ordered a shirt for me with "I waited 12 years for this" on the front and "Baptism 10-19-22" on the back. Having my friend and spiritual mentor baptize me made this one of the most amazing days of my life. It was worth the wait.

In short, Roger's work has touched me in a profound way many times whether he knew it or not, and I am forever grateful. He never ceases to amaze me with his tireless work to get the Lord's Word out to everyone. It's fun to see how truly happy that makes him.

—Darren Stanley

Visits Provided a Lifeline through the Love Shown to Him

The one-on-one visits that I received from the Rescued Not Arrested (RNA) Ministry have been a great and wonderful blessing in my life. Being incarcerated has been the most traumatic experience of my life. I had never been in any kind of trouble before, and this experience was a very frightening time for me. When I was told about the RNA visits, I was uplifted and thought, "Well, maybe this would be a nice experience and will help me through this traumatic time." I really had no idea that these visits would be such a great life-changing experience for me.

The first RNA visit I had was with Roger, who brought a real love and concern for where I was mentally, emotionally, and spiritually. That first meeting was a very uplifting experience for me and showed me a deeper and more sincere love from God through Roger than I had seen in a very long time on a personal basis. During my thirty-five years of marriage, and during my years of attending church and being a Christian, I do not recall anyone making it a point to just stop and visit to see how I was doing and help with any needs or minister to me with God's love. These visits reaffirmed what I knew, but took for granted – that God loves even me and that I am forever important to Him.

Roger brought such a peaceful, yet strong spirit into the visits that I was comforted right away. The love and charisma that came from him was an undeniable testimony to God's love and how He will use us if we let Him. Roger came bringing a spirit of comfort and encouragement that could only be from God, and he always had a message from the Bible for me to dwell on and build upon to get closer to God.

I have met with two other members of RNA and received messages and blessings from God's Word by them to strengthen me in my Christian walk. God knew more about my needs than I did, and He provided these men to help uplift me in the time of my needs. All of these visits were anointed and blessed by God and confirmed that He needed to get my attention and rescue me from just being a complacent "Sunday Christian."

I never thought much about jail and prison ministry before, but now I see how important it is and how much it touches the lives of incarcerated people like me. This field of harvest is being passed by and ignored, even though it could be the easiest harvest due to the concentration of hurting and lost people. These visits have shown me a need that is not being met by most churches and Christians in our communities.

The Bibles provided are a great blessing, and in some cases will become a lifesaver because they are the only introduction to God that the inmate has had. We cannot grow closer to God without His message of instruction, encouragement, and love. The life application study portion of the Bible helps us immensely in understanding and applying God's Word to our daily lives.

As Luke 19:10 says, Christ came to earth on a search-and-rescue mission. We have the opportunity and invitation to be a part of His search-and-rescue team. We would never find our way to Him in our own power or in our own nature, so the RNA ministry is the lifeblood of our mission to these lost sheep of His.

—Allen

Transformed in Lockdown

I am thirty-one years old. I was born in Mexico, but I have resided in the United States for twenty-six years. I currently find myself incarcerated at the Federal Detention Center in Seattle, Washington. This is my testimony about the Rescued Not Arrested Holy Bible. That book has transformed my life, my way of thinking, and my way of worshipping the Lord.

I remember the first days after I entered the prison. We were on a COVID quarantine for almost thirty days without books to read. We had no rec, no phones, nothing – except being in a cell twenty-four hours a day. I have to say I consider myself very lucky, or maybe that was just God wanting me to know Him better. One day at lunch time an inmate worker who was feeding the unit handed me the Rescued Not Arrested Holy Bible and told me to read it. Although I had read the Bible several times, I still had difficulty understanding what our purpose in life is.

Through the Scriptures, I've regained trust, and my faith has surpassed any obstacle that has come my way. I have to admit that after I started reading the Holy Bible, I learned that God doesn't make mistakes. He, through His Son, Jesus Christ, has shown me mercy and a compassionate love that has changed me deeply inside and out. Today, thanks to God's Word, I have received Christ in my life, and I consider myself a born-again Christian. I might not be super intelligent or super wise in regard to knowing the Bible just yet, but up to this date, it has changed me into a better man, a better father, a better husband, and a better son.

The Lord has called me to join His army, and I will follow Him regardless of the current situation that I'm facing. I pray that the Holy Bible keeps transforming lives like it has transformed mine. I pray that through Christ's sacrifice and God's infinite love and power, we can one day move mountains.

—J. G. in Seattle

Tried, Convicted, and Rescued

I was tried and convicted of two class 4 felonies the same year my son was diagnosed with terminal lung cancer. I was sentenced to four years of probation, but at the end of that, my son was put into a medically induced coma and pronounced gravely ill. The next day, my father passed away. The chaplain told me I needed to have faith.

During this time, I violated my probation. I couldn't pay my fines and couldn't find the money for my weekly urine samples. The judge issued a warrant for my arrest, and I was to turn myself in. I knew I was headed to prison, but I wanted to see my kids back East first, which I was able to do.

When the transportation company came to pick me up to take me back to Arizona, the chaplain brought me the Rescued Not Arrested Bible. That was the day God started working on my heart. Six days and six different jails, and all I had was my Rescued Not Arrested Bible. All those nights God worked on me, giving me verse after verse about faith and obedience, death and grief, and restoration. But most importantly, I read verses about how to heal.

I arrived in Arizona on a Monday. My Bible was taken away from me, but they couldn't take God's promises from me. Throughout the next month, wherever I was taken, I was able to find the verses I needed in a new Rescued Not Arrested Bible. When I arrived at Perryville Prison and was processed, I was led to my cell – alone. After the door slammed behind me, there it was again – a Rescued Not Arrested Bible, worn and tattered, but waiting for me.

As I look back, I laugh. I feel that the Rescued Not Arrested Ministry followed me from Pennsylvania to an Arizona prison. When I am released, God's patience and forgiveness are going with me. I was so excited when I found out that as a participant of Governor Ducey's Second Chance Program, I would get a chance to meet Roger Munchian, the founder of the Rescued Not Arrested Ministry. I had time to read his book and could relate to him on his journey to find Christ. I didn't just get to meet Roger once, though. I met with him three more times when he gave my fellow inmates and me information about necessary resources upon release; but most importantly, he gave us hope.

I sincerely thank the RNA Ministries and donors who are working diligently to spread God's message to me and other prisoners like me, giving us light on some of our darkest days.

—Teresa A. Gerald

Regaining the Will to Live in Prison

Thank you for reaching out to us inmates. Your ministry, with the help of our Lord, saved my life. I'm doing a nine-and-a-half-month sentence right now. This is my second time in prison. I was out for only four months when the county revoked my probation and put me back in here for failing a drug test.

After my first three years of incarceration, I was happy to return to freedom and to be reunited with my wife and kids. I found a good job and was trying very hard to leave my sinful ways behind, but my addiction was stronger than me, and I started to get high. On October 6, 2022, I had a court appointment, and they decided to test me right there in court. I failed, and they put me back in jail. My world came crashing down on me that day. I lost everything again, including my marriage, my job, my family support, and my freedom. It was bone-crushing for me.

I never before felt as I felt during the next month. I was very depressed, and the pain was so strong that it sucked all the strength from my body. I lost all my will to live. The only reason I didn't take my life was that I didn't have the strength to get up, but I prayed every day for God to take me away.

One day I was standing in front of the book cart, on autopilot, reading the titles of books. I had no intention of actually choosing a book to read, but I saw the title on one Bible on that book cart that said, "Rescued Not Arrested." It got my attention. I grabbed hold of that Bible, and I'm never going to let it out of my hands – ever. That night, my prayers changed from wanting to die to "Please God, save me." And He heard me! My life is still a mess. My family still won't talk to me at all. I'm still in prison, and I still live with the consequences of all my sins. However, for the first time in my life, I feel hope and real peace inside me. I feel the presence of Jesus every day and I experience the power of His Word in my life. It's working a miracle in me. I hope I can meet you in the future and tell you more about me and get to know you as well. I will pray that God keeps blessing your ministry so you keep on saving lives in prison. We sure need God's love and power in this place.

—Hector Estein

A Four-Year Journey from Suicidal to Saved

For four years, I had been labeled, criticized, chastised, and called a criminal and a felon. I was not the worst person in the 4th Avenue Jail or the only one who had never before been behind prison gates, walls, and doors. This was demoralizing for me. I was there on a class 3 felony for a stalking, aggravated harassment charge and had been told by my attorney that I was looking at a minimum of seven to eleven years.

For all the allegations against me, I was not a criminal, and I had lived a productive, good life outside of this house – Satan's house, this house of hell and unsanitary disgust. I was caught up in a serious wave of emotions and in a serious deep depression with thoughts of how I could end my life.

I lost everything I had that was most precious to me, including my mother, whom I had cared for daily. I lost her house when I sold it to pay for attorneys. I lost my entire life savings. Everything I had worked for was gone. I was a failure in my mind and was merely a criminal and a number to Maricopa County. I thought I was faithful by believing in God and our Lord and Savior Jesus Christ. I was wrong. I had been arrested three times, and by November 2021, I had spent several holiday seasons in jail for the same thing.

I had gone through nine straight months of trauma in my life. My twenty-seven-year-old son told me he wanted nothing to do with me. My only sibling, my older brother, passed away from a massive brain bleed due to opioids. Then my uncle, who was my mentor and father figure, died unexpectedly from cancer. My girlfriend of six years dumped me due to me stalking her, in addition to my verbal abuse and my mental instability. I lost my best job ever, and the next month I found my mom bled out – ten-and-a-half pints of blood that looked like a murder scene.

I was a mess and a mental basket case. At this time, I was sentenced for my charges and went to jail for four months. I then got out on probation, but I violated the requirements of my probation and went back to 4th Avenue Jail for another four months. I spent sixty-seven days during COVID in a cell by myself – depressed, lost, and on the verge of suicide. I was a lost soul.

In December 2021, I read *Rescued Not Arrested*, and I knew I had to meet Roger Munchian. I was looking for help. I requested to meet Roger, but was told he was busy. I read the Bible daily and did Bible studies in the pod with others. Marcus led the studies. He was an older man and met with me every day because he knew I was in a deep depression. I finally met Roger, and he could see I was in a bad way. He told me then that he was there for me, and that with the help of the Lord and my will, I would be okay. I cried my eyes out, sharing my case and how I felt.

Roger never made me feel wrong or that what I was feeling was false or untrue. He could see that the devil was fighting to keep me from being one of God's children. That night after I was locked down in my cell, I let it all go. I told the Lord that He could take me and do His will with me. I asked Him to guide me, believe in me, help me, and break the chains that were holding me down. I asked Him to remove all the thoughts of suicide and death completely away. I asked for forgiveness for all my wrongs and sins against everyone and against myself.

I wanted to feel our Lord and Savior come over my life. I wanted to feel the power of God and the joy of being saved. I woke up the next morning, not even sure of what happened after my prayers the night before. All I knew was that I felt like a completely different man. I had a sense of a relief and security and an overwhelming feeling of the Lord in my life. I don't know what would have happened if I had not been introduced to RNA, had not met Roger, and did not have his help with his prayers, guidance, support, and feeling of caring and love. Roger and RNA guided my journey back to God's right hand, leading me to be saved. I was baptized February 11th, 2023 by Roger himself, one of the best days of my life.

Reading *Rescued Not Arrested* led me to Roger and to my Lord and Savior Jesus Christ. I know that meeting Roger, reading his story, and having him send me the teaching Bible (NIV Life Application Study Bible) saved me from the doom of the devil and from taking my own life. It was the Lord's hand helping me, and I have Roger Munchian to thank for all of it. Thank you, Roger and Rescued Not Arrested.

—James Itule, a true soldier of Christ

From Suicidal Thoughts to Living for God's Kingdom

It was October 2010. I was feeling far from rescued sitting in that tiny, cold, second-floor chapel in Maricopa County's 4th Avenue Jail. The pastor had us turn to Colossians 1:13-14. He explained that my life of sin had led to my predicament. "God rescued you!" he said. "He is giving you an opportunity for a new life of hope and purpose in Christ Jesus!"

Facing a potential twenty-eight years in prison and feeling suicidal, I gave my life to Christ and looked forward to those weekly services and one-on-ones with my pastor, Roger Munchian. I know he shuns titles and prefers to be called "brother," but I consider him the shepherd God sent to me.

Roger spoke to my heart. I remember messages of hope and purpose, of life service rather than lip service, and of true repentance that leads to true life change. Roger's ministry made sure we all had study Bibles. Week in and week out, he and his faithful volunteers taught us how to study and apply God's Word to our lives. Matthew 6:33-34 was taught: seek first His kingdom and His righteousness. Learn to hope and think eternally. Roger used Scripture passages to show us the way in regard to all the worries that a pre-sentenced inmate dwells on, as well as the upcoming court dates and the past life of failures and sin.

God is using Roger and his ministry team to reach the "least of these," even the worst of the worst whom most jail ministries and churches neglect. I am eternally grateful to my Lord and Savior Jesus Christ for putting a faithful man of God like Roger in my life. I am excited to read his book and see the path that led us to meeting in that cold, second-story chapel. I am even more excited to join Roger's ministry team one day, Lord willing.

January 2023 update. It has been nearly ten years since I wrote the above testimony for Roger's book. I now have the honor of updating my testimony for his new book.

I did eight years soft in the Arizona Department of Corrections, getting out on Christmas morning in 2020. During my time there, I kept in touch with Rescued Not Arrested and tithed to RNA every month, which was not easy since I worked with the yard crew and had very little income while store prices increased. But the Lord taught me faithful obedience. I stayed involved in the inmate-led ministry on the yard and took advantage of all classes and programs that were available to prepare for life on the outside, even if I could only learn one thing from them. I also asked God if I could be involved with RNA upon my release.

The Lord blessed my time in so many ways. I heard a pastor on TBN say that some men have to go to prison to get free. That was me. I had rejected all other lifelines from the Lord, so it was either prison or death. I am thankful for my time in prison.

Today I work full time for a company that Roger referred me to – a second-chance company. I live in a Christian ministry home and am involved in Celebrate Recovery and AA. I am slowly regaining the trust of my family and friends whom I hurt so deeply in my past life. I am amazed at how God is redeeming and restoring my life, and I am privileged to spend time with those who have similar backgrounds. My probation team and therapist are important parts of the Lord's work in my life. Without clear boundaries and accountability that probation has set for me, I believe I would have gone back to my past life.

I have found a freedom within these boundaries that I never knew existed. I can look at myself in the mirror and be okay, knowing that I am under construction as long as I continue to seek the Lord and His will. As Paul said, *I have learned to be content* (Philippians 4:11); that is a wonderful place to be in a world of such discontent!

I encourage anyone who reads this to consider the simplicity of the gospel. We complicate it with religious rules and practices. I believe in faithful obedience to God's Word – not to gain God's salvation, but to be a good steward of it. The Bible tells us that Jesus is the Savior of the whole world and that there is no other name under heaven whereby we must be saved (Acts 4:12). It is so simple that I almost missed it.

Thanks to Roger and his wonderful volunteers and supporters who provided so much hope for me when I was incarcerated, but who also continue to inspire and help me on this next chapter of life. *Trust in the Lord with all your heart and lean not on your own understanding; in all your ways submit to him, and he will make your paths straight* (Proverbs 3:5-6).

—Kirk Holloway, shepherded by Christ and living for His kingdom

School Teacher and Coach Learns He Is God's Child, not a Modern-Day Leper

I was asked to go to the principal's office when my after-school duty was finished. The police were waiting to take me to the station for questioning. After they interrogated me in Buckeye Jail, they sent me to the Maricopa County 4th Avenue Jail to be processed.

I bonded out of jail and spent the next nine months working my way through the legal system. My sentencing date came, and I went from being Josh Jacobson, Liberty Elementary School District teacher and soccer coach, to "Sex Offender." The *Arizona Republic* clearly defined me in their headline: "Former Teacher to Be Sentenced for Sex Abuse." The world heard "sex offender." All I heard was "former teacher." My life's passion for educating youth and teaching the fundamentals of my lifeblood – soccer – was gone forever. I had become a member of today's equivalent of a leper in Jesus's time: sex offender.

Until I was arrested, I thought I was a good person. I never used illegal drugs, rarely drank alcohol, and always treated people kindly. I knew about God and believed in God, which led me to believe I was good enough to go to heaven. I was better than most people, right? Well, God answered that question loudly and clearly when my cell door slammed shut: No. The path I had chosen put me behind those bars, but God had a very different plan for my life.

In October of 2007, after I signed a plea deal, I was sentenced to nine months in Maricopa County Jail with lifetime probation. As I put on my Maricopa County Jail stripes, I realized that I could either make this next nine months the most miserable time of my life or I could use the time to do something positive with my life. The choice I made put me on a path to meet Jesus Christ face to face.

On New Year's Eve in 2007, I called my girlfriend. She told me that someone from the CCV was going to visit me, but she didn't know when. I had played on the CCV coed soccer team, but I didn't know who to expect with this visit or when. The very next morning, New Year's Day, I was taken out of the pod for a visit, which was strange since we only got visits on Wednesdays. I met Roger from the CCV prison ministry that day. This was the day of my first real face-to-face time with Jesus Christ.

We talked about my upbringing and my beliefs. I told Roger that I believed in God, which to me meant that I was in good with the Big Guy. Then he showed me what James 2:19 says: *You believe that there is one God. Good! Even the demons believe that – and shudder.* Roger also shared his testimony with me. I went back to the pod that day with a lot of questions and some deep self-examination of my life and choices. I prayed to Jesus, asked for forgiveness, and accepted Him as my Lord and Savior that night. My life plan changed 180 degrees that day, and I will never turn back.

Roger continued to minister to me for the rest of my sentence, but he didn't stop there. When I was released from jail, I knew that my newfound freedom opened up a lot of choices and limitless paths to take – most of them bad if I was not connected to godly people. Roger connected me to a Bible study group and to church so I could keep my feet firmly planted on His path and live out one of my favorite verses, John 15:5: *I am the vine; you are the branches. If you remain in me and I in you, you will bear much fruit; apart from me you can do nothing.*

I am now married to my beautiful wife, Maria, and we have two beautiful children who are true gifts from God. Yes, I will be a registered sex offender for the rest of my life. We use the term "modern-day leper" because our offenses are the only crimes that require us to forever wear a label of shame and to be shunned, even in most churches. I praise God that CCV is not one of those churches. My family has been welcomed as loved members of that congregation, and I am a co-leader of the same men's group that accepts all men in spite of their past. I give all glory to Jesus.

I cannot imagine where my life would be without Jesus and the people whom He has brought into my life. It took a nine-month jail sentence for me to become the man that God wanted me to be. Every day I do my best to understand His plan for my life and to live it out. I have to be intentional every day to pray and get into the Bible, but I have more peace now with my new perspective of this life being temporary because my life is not my own.

Thank you to those who minister in the devil's land of jail and prison. I want to give a special big thank you to Roger Munchian and his God-given passion and vision.

2023 update: I have been working as a framer for almost eleven years. Five years ago, I moved up from being a laborer to an assistant superintendent. I have been married for thirteen years. I'm still serving out my lifetime probation sentence, and though it hasn't been easy, God continues to bless me daily. I believe that comes from doing my best to honor Him each and every day.

—Josh Jacobson

A Message of Hope from Roger Munchian's Daughter to the Kids and Family of Those Who Are Incarcerated

(Rachel Munchian is the infant Roger is hold-ing in the picture from Lewis Prison)

My mom always told me that the day I was born was a rainy, gloomy day with terrible weather. I'm sure it would have felt a little less gloomy if my dad would have been able to make it to the hospital. My dad had only been in prison for seven months by the time I was born. My mom, grandparents, and even little Andrew all celebrated the joyous occasion, but the family was not complete without my dad.

Although I spent the first year and a half of my life without seeing my dad daily, my life – even before his release – had been nothing but a blessing. To this day, our family remains joyful, healthy, and whole, and I have God to thank for providing healing and restoration in my family's life. I truly believe that through his faith in God, my dad was able to break the generational curse that seemed to plague my family: first from the Armenian genocide, then from the Soviet oppression, and lastly, from alcoholism and the brutality that a life of crime can offer. Now my brother, my two sisters, and I live happy, fulfilling lives and have grown up with the church.

Although I have always known my dad's story, I have never really been able to register that the "insane Roger Rabbit" and my dad were the same person. God has changed my dad's life so significantly that he has become unrecognizable from his past. I'm sharing this story because I want others to know that restoration and salvation is possible in everyone's life, no matter what the circumstances may be.

For those who have loved ones who may be currently serving time or who are caught up in a life of crime, I want you to know that there is always hope that God can alter the course of their lives and bring them peace and healing. Thanks to my father's decision to walk with God, my family and I have been able to experience God's blessing of peace and restoration, and my prayer is that all families who may be suffering will be able to accept the healing that God has to offer them. Don't ever give up. Keep trusting God with your loved ones.

—Rachel Munchian

Epilogue

A Personal Message from Roger

As I look back, I can see the miracles that God worked in my life. For many years, I refused to acknowledge Him, but He loved me enough to show me His strength and His trustworthiness.

- My family was saved from genocide.

- A friend from the Gulag was able to enter us in the lottery for American visas.

- I survived the beating from Hondo and the Armenian Power.

- I survived the shoot-out with Hondo and the AP.

- I survived flipping my Mustang and skidding across the desert upside down.

- I survived flying through the windshield and crashing my Nissan truck.

- My passengers and I survived the 1997 accident.

- My federal cases were dismissed.

- My bail was reduced in the state cases.

- I was granted permission to go to Armenia while awaiting sentencing.

- My sentence was reduced. What could have been 150 years was reduced to two years.

- I was given two weeks freedom before incarceration.

- I was able to retrieve a Bible upon entering the Lewis prison.

- I did not receive the customary beating for dissing the yard leadership in prison.

- The cartel leaders have allowed me to live after I pulled out of the drug scene.

- RNA prison ministry has remained 100 percent volunteer with no fundraising.

These miracles, my experiences, and the Bible, along with the guidance of the Holy Spirit, brought me to God's truth. I became a new man and learned many lessons. Some of these are:

- God is real. He isn't just sitting on the sidelines. He tries to get our attention.

- Until we believe that what we believe is really real, we cannot commit to live by it.

- The Bible is true. It was written in three languages on three continents by forty authors over a period of fifteen hundred years and covered a period of four thousand years. Fulfilled prophecy, history, and science have confirmed the truthfulness and authenticity of its message.

- A true believer, a true Christian, is different from a labeled Christian. We receive labels at birth, but it takes a second birth to make us a Christian.

- Man-made traditions and ceremonies of most denominations do not have a basis in the Bible, and they often misdirect people into trusting those things instead of God.

- Altar calls and the sinner's prayer served a purpose at one time when people's word was their bond. They brought a salvation message to the common people and gave them the opportunity to choose to trust Christ. Today, though, they often give a false hope of salvation with no change in people's lives because their word is no longer their bond.

- As scripture permits, toxic relationships and former activities must be abandoned. At the same time, positive relationships, mentors, and good influences must be formed in order to live a successful new life.

- God offers hope and the ability to break the cycle of crime and poverty.

- Salvation is free for all who will believe and trust in Jesus Christ – even after many mistakes and failures.

"Rescued Not Arrested" is actually a paradox, but my whole life seems to be filled with paradoxes. Some of these are the result of my Damascus Road experience, and some come from the miracles

God worked in my life and in the lives of my family. I went from one extreme to another, such as from:

- Siberian oppression to American freedom to real freedom in Christ

- Poverty to opportunity

- Despair to hope

- Doubt and skepticism to belief and trust

- Speeding down the highway to death and hell to heading to eternity in heaven

- Crime to Christ

- Serving self to serving God

- Love of money and power to love for Christ

- Trafficking tons of marijuana nationwide to trafficking tons of Bibles internationally

- Living in a country with no opportunity to advance to living in freedom and being truly blessed with a wife of twenty-two years and four healthy children, all at the top of their class, and one who became valedictorian

Yes, God rescues. God restores. God redeems. God saves. God blesses. This is the process for God's method of rescue, and I can relate to each step. God used my Mercedes and a concrete barrier wall to rescue me. I responded to His call as He restored me, but God refined me with bankruptcy and a harsh legal system; then He delivered me from the incarceration of both prison and myself. Just as Christ taught Paul after his Damascus Road event without the aid of the other apostles, He took me aside and redeemed, saved, and taught me through His Word without the aid of other pastors, teachers, or schools of thought from any denominational tradition. He handed me a vision to reach the least of these behind bars and to challenge the church to not categorize sin, but to love and forgive all sinners. God has been blessing me with my family and my ministry as He provides beyond anything I could have hoped or imagined.

Just like the day the doctor had to re-break my leg and fix it the right way, how many times have we ignored the Master Surgeon and relied on our own healing? Every time God allows our bad choices to re-break us, it causes more pain and healing than He had intended. He is a jealous God – jealous for you. He is eternal and wants to spend eternity with you, and He will do whatever it takes to bring you back to Him because once those doors slam shut at the end of time, it will be too late. God does not want a single one of His children to be eternally lost. He is more concerned about our eternal status than our status on earth. He will allow anything into our lives to get our attention in hope of rescuing us from eternal damnation.

If you are reading this and have never yielded your life to Jesus Christ, don't you think it's time to listen to His call? Don't you think it's time to use the circumstances, the chains that bind you now, to be set free by His perfect love – by the blood that Jesus shed for you?

If you believe you are a Christian, if you've said those words of acceptance of Christ, but still feel the conviction of sin in your life, it is time to finally ask yourself the hard questions: Am I a Christian in name only? Am I a labeled Christian?

I was a labeled Christian from birth to age twenty-five, professing to be a Christian because I was born in a Christian country. It took complete wreckage and death before I realized the destructiveness of living such a lie. You may be like me – professing to be a Christian because of your heritage or an emotional moment in your past when you answered an altar call or repeated the "sinner's prayer," but have never really committed your life to understanding the truth of God's Word and obeying it.

So where are you today? Ask yourself: What is truth? What do you believe? What is your purpose in life? Has God brought you to a place where you have lost everything? Have you seen that you have no hope without Him? Is the intensity of the darkness around you beyond what you can bear? If so, realize that this is not God's judgment; this is God's love calling you. His desire is to write His story in your life, starting today. God promises, *I will instruct you and teach you in the way you should go; I will counsel you with my loving eye on you* (Psalm 32:8).

My friend, you can be rescued, restored, and redeemed by the blood of Jesus. Your Damascus moment will come, bringing the dawn of a new beginning. You can have a bright future living in the eternal light of Jesus Christ.

Thank you for reading my book. Now please let me pray for you:

> *Father God, thank You for the breath of life You just granted us this second; we take that for granted too often. Please bless this child with physical, emotional, and spiritual healing. Lord, please deliver this child from the strongholds of this world and renew their heart and mind with the transformative power of the Holy Spirit right now. Please put a deep hunger in their heart to desire to know You and Your truth like never before. Protect, provide, and guide their steps with Your healing hands to a place of peace and joy that only You can provide and that comes from above.*
>
> *In the name of Jesus Christ, our Lord and Savior, I pray this. Amen!*

Please write to us and request a free Bible and a mentor to begin your journey – searching, seeking, and knocking for the truth. We would love to hear how my story helped your story become a part of God's story.

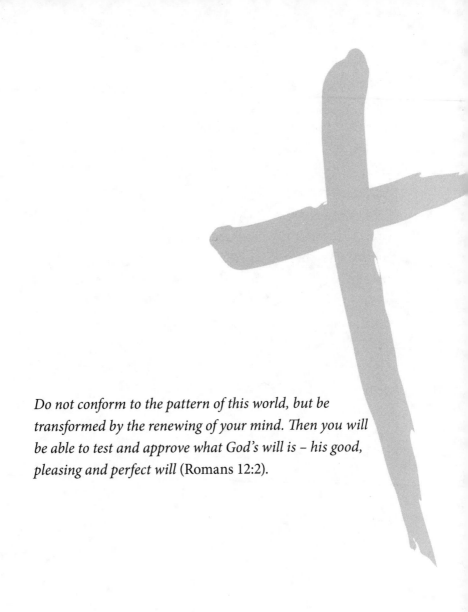

Do not conform to the pattern of this world, but be transformed by the renewing of your mind. Then you will be able to test and approve what God's will is – his good, pleasing and perfect will (Romans 12:2).